# Still Here

## A MEMOIR OF LOVE, LOSS, AND TRIUMPH AFTER STILLBIRTH

WRITTEN BY:

# Alishia Anderson

Published by Ali Ande Enterprise LLC

**ISBN:** 978-1-7325825-0-7 (Paperback)

Cover design by Gabriel Akinrinmade (Boxofwolves.com).

Book edited by Morshe Araujo.

Book printed by CreateSpace, An Amazon.com Company, in the United States of America.

First Edition 2018.

aliandeenterprise@gmail.com

www.aliandeenterprise.com

*I want to dedicate this book to my handsome sleeping angel, Derrek Jerrell Anderson Jr., and to all the other sleeping angels, unidentified blessings, and precious babies/children that have lost their lives. I pray this book is one of many ways that I can keep your legacy alive, and a way to help and comfort other grieving parents (and families) experiencing the same pain and emptiness of losing a child as your daddy and I experienced losing you. Although you were only with us for twenty-eight short weeks, you forever changed our lives. I am forever indebted to you and the huge impact you've imprinted upon my heart. Thank you, son, for teaching me how to truly live and love! I love you with all my mind, heart, and soul. Until we meet again...in the words of Robert Munsch "I'll love you forever, I'll like you for always, long as I'm living my baby you'll be!"*

*With my deepest love,*

*Mommy*

# Contents

# Introduction

## The Facts About Losing A Child

*"Do not fear, for I am with you;*
*Do not anxiously look about you,*
*for I am your God I will strengthen you,*
*surely, I will help you,*
*Surely I will uphold you*
*with My righteous right hand."*
*– **Isaiah 41:10**, New American Standard Bible*

There is nothing that can mentally, physically, or emotionally prepare you for the loss of a child, especially a young child, a child that was born still, or a child you didn't even get a chance to meet or see. All three scenarios are equally tragic and equally difficult to deal with. While I have not personally experienced miscarriage or infant loss, I can identify with the pain associated with losing a child through stillbirth. Nothing about the process is something I would wish upon anyone anticipating the birth of a child or multiple children. Gaining the title of grieving parent, no matter how young or old the child, is no club any parent would willingly sign up for.

But the truth is, far more people than we are aware of suffer from the loss of a child, and usually in silence. Before I lost my son, I only thought of losing a child during pregnancy, during birth, or in the early years of infancy as a rare occurrence. But after reluctantly gaining membership into this fetal mortality club, I realized that far too many men, women, and families suffer from the loss of a child, brother, sister, grandchild, niece, nephew, cousin, godchild etc., more than we think.

There is a veil of silence that accompanies the loss of a child. For those in the early stages of pregnancy, you may suffer in silence because you haven't even shared the news that you were expecting to your loved ones and friends, so you are tasked with dealing with the tragedy of losing your precious baby on your own. Or just as you were getting excited about the prospect of spreading the good news about your new nine-month passenger, you receive the news that your baby can no longer be detected via ultrasound or by using a heart Doppler. I'm sure suffering in silence brings upon its own challenges. Similarly, you've made your announcement "Facebook official", and you've had your gender reveal party only to receive the news that your baby no longer has a detectable heartbeat. You absorb the initial shock as a wave of grief showers over you like a tsunami.

Maybe you've witnessed your child's birth, held your baby in your arms, received flowers, cards, and celebratory gifts in your baby's honor only to have your child ripped from your life days, weeks, months, or even a few years later due to illness or some fluke happenstance. With all instances of fetal and/or child loss, grief is an individualized bid. Typically, the journey starts off with a swell of condolences, prayers, well-wishes, visits, and much more support, but as the novelty of loss "wears off", you are often left alone to suffer in silence. Although people truly mean well, they tend to "move on" with their regularly scheduled lives while you're stuck trying to reassemble the shattered pieces of your life.

As I have transparently shared my ups and downs, joys and pains, heartaches and triumphs of the loss of my son, I've realized how isolating stillbirth can be. It occurred to me that prior to my own first-hand experience of losing my child, I never really encountered someone up-close and personal who had experienced the loss of a child (or so I thought). But after our horrific ordeal, people began to come out the woodwork in droves with countless stories of their personalized loss, tragedy, and triumph. It was at those very moments I realized many families suffer in silence after the loss of their children. I didn't want to be silent about my experience.

Talking about my loss truly helped with *my* grieving process. I shouted from the rooftops about my son any chance I got. I wrote about him in my journal, I posted statuses about my progression with stillbirth on Facebook, I used my fashion blog as a platform to chronicle my journey, I had heart-to-hearts with my husband in regard to our angel and spoke to various family members and friends on how I felt about my loss. I made it known that DJ was, still is, and will always be a part of the fabric of our lives. I go out of my way to remind people of his existence, because he was a real person, who truly lived within me. Even though my husband and I were the only ones in the room to witness the one pound, 5.30 ounces of chocolatey goodness that was my son, I still try to make him apart of my daily conversation. He is apart of me like I am apart of him. We are one!

The format of this book is set up as a memoir. It is my firsthand account of losing our first child through stillbirth. While this book was written as a part of my healing process at various stages throughout my grief journey, I really wrote it as a manuscript to help countless others going through parallel experiences of child loss. There is no easy entry point into this club. You are shoved into the deep end and expected to learn to swim on the fly, while trying to keep your head above water. You can easily lose your mind or find yourself in a never-ending spiral of sadness, depression, anger, and much more if you don't have something or someone to anchor your grief to. For me, my personal anchor was God! I am a Christian. My dad is a Pastor, so I grew up in the church all my life. I knew who God was on paper. I've heard, read, and sung about Him for thirty-plus years, but it wasn't until my own stillbirth experience that I truly had to exercise the faith I had so often read about in the Bible. I had to truly learn how to wholeheartedly rely on God, His strength and power as my source to fuel me and keep me going from day to day.

Throughout this book, you will see many elements of my faith and relationship with God incorporated. If you are not a Christian or do not believe in any divine higher power, I don't mean to offend you. But I must confess my faith in God and my personal relationship with Him truly is the secret to how I was able to get through this tragic ordeal in one piece. It is how I can talk about my angel without breaking down, or how I can share my experience of tragedy with millions of people and have a heart filled with gratitude for the short yet impactful life of my son, with a smile on my face.

At the beginning of each chapter you will find a Bible verse. I am praying you will use these verses to: 1.)

Remember God is always with us even at our lowest moments, 2.) Reflect inward and chronicle your experience through journaling, and 3.) Carry with you as a personal pick-me-upper on those days when you feel like you cannot go on.

I want to use this book as a launch pad to open dialogue about the loss of a child. I want you to understand that you are not alone, that while I wish we met through different circumstances, you can conquer the defeat and setback from this life altering situation. Use this book to help you sort out your grief, acknowledge the person you are becoming after the loss of your baby, establish your new normal, find ways to honor your baby after loss while taking care of your spouse, partner, other children, family and friends, but most importantly yourself. You can get through this tough time! You will come out on the other side of grief victorious. Just because you are down and out doesn't mean you have to stay there. I'm speaking love and life over your current situation. In the end, I know that you will come out as a conqueror! So, let's embark on this journey hand-in-hand, side-by-side, page-by-page down the road to recovery.

# Chapter 1

## The Joys Of Pregnancy

*"And on that day, they offered great sacrifices and rejoiced because God had given them great **joy**, even the women and children rejoiced, so that the **joy** of Jerusalem was heard from afar."*
*– **Nehemiah 12:43**, New American Standard Bible*

### In the Beginning

No single experience is more life changing than discovering you have a little human growing inside of you. From the first time your pregnancy test shows a plus sign or two double lines confirming you're indeed pregnant, your entire world changes. The thought of becoming responsible for another human's life, one who fully depends on you for their survival, is one of life's most magical journeys. The weight of this tremendous assignment can bring on a wave of emotions ranging from excitement, confusion, nervousness, wonder, amazement, fear, and much more.

I found out I was expecting our first child when I decided to take an at-home pregnancy test one Sunday evening in August 2015. I took the test because something within me hinted that I might be pregnant. As I waited patiently for my results, a wave of anticipation rolled over me. My palms were sweaty, and my heart pounded. After the longest two minutes of my life, the results finally appeared. Two double lines! It took a moment to reconcile that two lines meant I was carrying a life. My husband; however, wasn't so sure about the positive result, because one of the lines was faint. In his skepticism, he suggested I schedule a doctor's appointment to verify the at-home test was accurate. When I went to my doctor's appointment, they had me provide a urine sample and within minutes the nurse revealed what I knew all along. I was indeed pregnant.

At that very moment, excitement rushed over my body. My husband and I had been married for three years. Ever since the day we walked down the aisle and said our "I Do's," we'd been bombarded with the questions… *"So, when do you plan on having kids?"* or *"when are you going to start a family?"* **SIDEBAR**: Can we talk about how inappropriate it is to ask someone when they plan to start having children? What if the couple has been trying but keeps running into complications while trying to conceive, or what if one of the partners is barren or sterile and can't get pregnant, or better yet, what if the couple simply doesn't want children? Bottom line: it is no one else's business when you plan to have children unless you feel comfortable sharing that information with them. This line of questioning should be eradicated from people's minds immediately!

To be honest, I never really spent much time thinking about becoming a mom. Of course, I loved to see adorable babies as I scrolled through my Instagram timeline and imagined picking out outfits for a munchkin I would one day call my own, but it just seemed like a fun little fantasy. My hubby and I played the *"how many kids do you want game,"* from time-to-time, but we never concretely had a plan as to when we wanted to start having children. So, the news I was pregnant was a bit of a shock to both of us but a much-welcomed surprise.

As I began my journey of preparing for the little bean growing inside me, I would sit back and wonder what he or she would be like, who he or she would look like, what type of personality he or she would have, along with all the other glorious things that come along with parenthood. After receiving the news confirming our pregnancy, I wanted to shout from the roof tops that I was expecting. However, my husband quickly reeled me in. He told me that I needed to wait until we reached the second trimester before we spread the news. I adhered to my husband's suggestion, but it was a torturous mission keeping this massive secret from my parents, siblings, in-laws, extended family, and close friends for thirteen weeks.

We read a lot of books and articles and heard from our doctor that the first thirteen weeks are critical weeks for fetal development. We closely followed all the medical instructions and advice, so we could move on to our second trimester without a hitch. In the crux of our waiting to spill the beans, we had our first prenatal appointment at seven weeks when we saw our little bean for the first time. We didn't know at the time that it was a boy, but to see the little flicker of his heartbeat made everything real. That tiny flutter of his heart instantly melted and stole mine. You never know that type of love for someone until you are expecting. For the next six to seven weeks, my husband and I talked, sang, read, and prayed with the baby every night as we became accustomed to officially thinking of our family expanding from two to three.

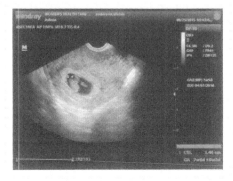

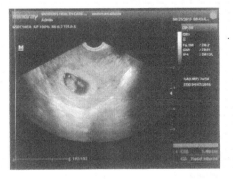

*The first time we saw our little bean at our seven-week ultrasound.*

I was bursting at the seams when it was finally time to announce we were growing our family. For our immediate family, I cut out little onesies on colorful cardstock paper and wrote *"I can't wait to meet you [insert family members name i.e. grandma, granddad, uncle, aunt etc.] Love Baby Anderson (coming Spring 2016)*. I then filled manila envelopes with confetti and a small bag of candy baby bottles and pacifiers that were sent to our parents, siblings, and grandparents. Our families were beyond excited to receive the wonderful news that we were finally starting a family.

My parents already had seven grandchildren at the time (three granddaughters, four grandsons) and they were thrilled to hear that they would be the proud grandparents of grandbaby number eight! My husband's family was super excited because this was going to be the first grandchild on his side of the family. Once we shared the news with our immediate families, the news spread like wildfire. I sent all my close friends a text message with a picture of a onesie with the same words inscribed on the front panel...*I can't wait to meet you [insert name and title] Love Baby Anderson (coming Spring 2016)*. We were flooded with well-wishes, love, and an overload of excitement.

I hit the beginning of my second trimester around the second week of October, and my husband gave me the green light to make our announcement on Facebook and Instagram that we were carrying a bundle of joy - we all know that nothing is "official" until you post it on Facebook! We took a picture of a pair of my husband's tan boots, a pair of my tan high-heel boots, and a tan pair of moccasins I ordered for our little bundle of joy with the caption, "Our family is growing by 2 feet, coming 2016." We received so many well-wishes that day. I was overwhelmed by the amount of love and enthusiasm we received from announcing that our family would be expanding!

*The official announcement we used on Facebook*
*to share we were adding a new family member to the Anderson unit.*

Just looking at our announcement brings a smile to my face. It was a time of pure joy. One that will NEVER be forgotten.

Baby Anderson
13 WEEKS
10.4.15

*Pregnancy photo captured at thirteen weeks*
*showing off my newly formed baby bump for the first time.*

After the news of Baby Anderson was out, I could finally commence with my regularly scheduled program. I began preparing for him (I still didn't know his gender at the time) and all that was to come. When I found out I was pregnant, I was one semester away from graduating from Kennesaw State University, in Marietta, Georgia with my second Bachelor's in Apparel Textile Technology. If I haven't mentioned it already, I am obsessed with fashion! I used the end of my second to last semester of fashion school planning for Baby Anderson's arrival and trying to figure out how to plan accordingly for school as I was scheduled to take my Senior Business Project course the following semester. This would occupy a huge chunk of my time, as it was a culmination of all the fashion and business courses I had taken the previous two years.

My husband and I found out we were having a boy at our twenty-week ultrasound appointment. That was the first time we got to see him on the huge monitor. He was such a relaxed baby. He was faced down with his spine positioned upward. But we could see his face, his hands, and his third leg, indicating we were having a boy. His feet were tap dancing on my bladder, hence the reason I had so many frequent trips to the restroom. We even heard his loud and strong heartbeat; something I cherish now even more. The day of my twenty-week ultrasound was probably one of the highlights of my seven-month pregnancy! I wish the joy that rushed over my husband and me that day could be packaged up in a bottle. It was simply a magical experience.

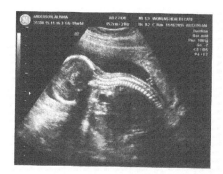 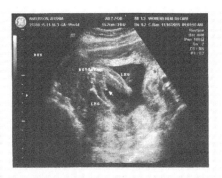

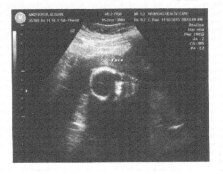

*DJ's twenty-week ultrasound.* **Top Left**: *Shown facing spine up.*
**Top Right**: *His bottom, legs, and third leg.*
**Bottom Center**: *His face is shown.*

Once we knew we were having a boy, we started planning our Gender Reveal Party. With the help of my close friend Ashley and input from my husband, we put together an awesome day for family and friends to guess Baby DJ's gender. No one knew his gender at the time except for my husband and I. Ashley, our co-party planner didn't even know. People were trying to get us to spill the beans, but we kept an air tight lid on the operation. My husband and I really weren't even supposed to know, but at the very last second in the ultrasound we decided together we would find out the sex of the baby and have everyone else guess.

*Our gender reveal recap of the amazing party we threw in DJ's honor.*

*The happy parents to be and the baby bump!*

The Gender Reveal party was filled with love, happiness, excitement, and bliss. We had family and friends travel from near and far to celebrate the life and gender reveal of DJ with us. It was amazing to see how much he was loved, even without anyone in that room besides myself and my husband ever getting a glimpse of him.

There were approximately five weeks in between our Gender Reveal Party and the day our worlds changed forever. As they say, what a difference a day can make. No words rang truer.

## Our Story; The Dark Side Of Pregnancy

> *"Set me like a seal upon your heart,*
> *like a seal upon your arm;*
> *for love is as strong as death..."*
> **– Song of Solomon 8:6**, *New American Standard Bible*

### Earth Shaking News

I can remember it like it was yesterday. It was a Friday, January 15, 2016 to be exact. I went to my doctor's office, accompanied by my husband, Derrek, for a routine ultrasound. During this visit, we were going to check and see if I had developed gestational diabetes during my pregnancy. I had just finished downing the sugary chilled drink the doctor's office provided when I was called back by the technician to conduct my ultrasound at twenty-eight weeks. We were so excited to see our baby boy again because it had been eight long weeks since we last discovered his gender. My husband called it from the day

I announced my pregnancy to him that we would be having a little boy. He knew in his heart he would finally have the junior he had been patiently waiting for, for four years of marital bliss.

As the ultrasound technician lifted my shirt and spread the cold gel on my protruding tummy, she began to locate my little munchkin while my husband and I awaited with quiet anticipation to see the life growing inside me. As she slowly showed shots of his tiny body she nonchalantly (probably as a way to not alarm us) mentioned that there wasn't a lot of fluid around him. I wasn't too sure what that meant, so I blissfully continued to look at the screen to get an exclusive sneak peak of my growing baby boy. When she scanned my son's head (which my husband later told me only measured in at twenty-four centimeters, a month behind his twenty-eight-week developing frame), she again mentioned there wasn't a lot of fluid around my baby. When I asked her what that meant she simply replied, "it's not good!"

I was dumbfounded by the answer but still didn't think too much of the technician's answer. Then she said, "I want the doctor to take a look at you." She briskly left the room while my husband and I anxiously awaited their return. When she left, I had an eerie feeling that something was wrong, but my hubby told me not to panic or overreact, and to wait until we heard an official analysis from the doctor. When the ultrasound technician came back into the room she silently cleaned the cold gel off my stomach, dropped my shirt to cover my belly, and escorted my husband and I across the hall to a new room where two doctors awaited our arrival.

At this point, I knew something wasn't right because during our first ultrasound there wasn't so much fanfare surrounding the status of our little pumpkin. What we heard spew from the doctor's mouth were seven words I never imagined in my wildest dreams I would hear. "*We could no longer detect a heartbeat.*" And just like that, in a matter of twenty minutes, our lives changed forever. As the doctor uttered those dreadful words, everything else seemed to go in slow motion. I was in total shock. The first reaction to the news was repeatedly telling my husband how sorry I was my body let DJ down and that I couldn't protect him. I knew Derrek had been super excited, as had I after some convincing, to pass down his name to our firstborn son and that honor was being stripped away instantaneously. The doctors excused themselves to give us some privacy to react to the nuclear bomb that was dropped in our laps. When they closed the door, I released the most piercing ball of emotion generated from the depths of my soul. All I could do was cry in the arms of my husband. He held me tightly and told me it was out of our control and in God's hands.

As I sat in the office motionless, staring at the cream-colored walls, the doctors emerged back into the room. They calmly tried to comfort me and my husband by letting me know that I wasn't to blame for the loss of our son. At that very moment, they could not say what caused his heart to stop beating. They went on to explain that sometimes these unfortunate situations occur during pregnancy. I later learned that one in every 160 pregnancies, or 26,000 pregnancies annually ends in stillbirth each year in the United States, according to Katherine Harmon from the Scientific American (Harmon, 2011), and I had just become a statistic.

The doctors also mentioned that we would always be the parents to this precious human being and that the road ahead of us would be tough and bumpy. But they encouraged us by letting us know that we would make it through if we leaned on one another and offered each other support, love, encouragement, strength, and time to grieve (in our own way) in our moments of weakness. The doctors briefly explained that I would have to deliver my deceased son. Then they presented me with several options: to be admitted to the hospital that same night, be admitted to the hospital sometime that weekend to be induced for labor or wait one to two weeks to let nature take its own course and allow my labor to occur on its own.

While waiting for DJ's labor to naturally begin on its own was a legit option my doctors did not recommend this alternative because they wanted me to avoid potential health risks associated with this delivery option. I didn't want to walk around knowing the child I was eagerly awaiting was trapped inside me, so I decided with the help of my hubby to get induced for labor on Saturday, January 16, 2016, one day after my devastating doctor's appointment.

### Home Sweet Home?

In the meantime, the doctors let us leave the office. I leaned on my husband to help muster up all the strength I possessed to exit the doctor's office in one piece. My husband and I drove to our house in separate cars. I literally don't even know how I managed to get behind the wheel of a vehicle in the disheveled state I was in. My mind was racing one hundred miles per minute, replaying the doctor's visit, and hearing those dreadful words replay in my mind over and over. *We couldn't detect a heartbeat.* When we got home, which seemed to take only seconds, we plopped on the couch and sat in silence as our disbelief and devastation drowned us. It is so crazy how you can plan, prep, and anticipate something or in our case, a person, and be told in an instant what you were waiting for was snatched away…never to return.

My husband and I decided we needed to spread the heartbreaking news to our immediate families. My husband put on his "papa bear" hat and took on the unsurmountable task of calling our parents one by one to inform them that the grandson they were so eagerly awaiting had gained his angel wings. Each of the calls was like detonating a bomb of agony onto our loved ones. After informing each parent, Derrek hung up the phone to let each of them deal with the news in their own way. Thankfully, our families did the rest of the heavy lifting and spread the word to our additional family members, immediate and extended, so we wouldn't have to recount the experience repeatedly while it was still so fresh. Once my husband finished calling our immediate families and I finished texting our close friends, we began to discuss the tragic news we received at the doctor's office. It was our way of coping with the situation at hand.

As followers of Christ, we decided we would lean on our faith and each other to help us navigate the murky waters of grief. The first thing we did was pray. My husband, who had been the strong rock up to this point, completely broke down into tears midway through his prayer. At that moment, I broke down too. All we could do was drown our sorrow with our tears. We stood in a quiet embrace as we learned the true meaning of grief, love, and loss.

As we talked about the next steps, I conducted an internet search: *"losing your baby at twenty-eight weeks."* That is when we first learned about the term stillbirth (or stillborn). Of course, you often hear about miscarriage which can occur anytime during the first trimester in pregnancy up through twenty weeks of gestation, but after we made it through our first trimester, we thought we were in the clear. Little did we know we would soon be inducted into a brother/sisterhood of parents who have lost their children through various stages of their pregnancy (miscarriage, stillbirth, or infant loss). While searching the internet I was blown away by the number of parents who experience this unfortunate happenstance every year, and the fact that we never even heard of the term stillbirth until we were experiencing it ourselves absolutely stunned me.

At this point we had more questions than answers. *How would they get my baby out? What would they do with him once he was out? Where would his body go? Would we get a chance to see him? Would we want to see him? Would we want to hold him? Who would he look like? How would my husband and I handle such a devastating blow?* All these things ran through our minds like a song on repeat. I searched for images of stillborn babies on the internet to "prepare" myself for what to expect when I saw my son for the first time.

After the dust settled that day, I retreated to my bedroom, pulled out my journal, and just began writing. I wrote and wrote and wrote, capturing my raw emotions until my hand got tired. Once I closed my journal, I whispered a silent prayer asking God for peace as we had to head to the hospital to deliver our baby boy early the next day. I prayed that God would comfort us in our darkest hour, and that he would bind us closer together as husband and wife, and mommy and daddy, so we could make the best decisions we could as parents for the angel we had been assigned.

Following my prayer, I showered, laid down and tried to mentally prepare for the next day. I literally thought I would report to the hospital, deliver my son, and go home all within a matter of two to three hours max. Clearly this was my first child because I was clueless about the journey I was about to embark upon. All I wanted was to try to make residence in a place of positivity, to find the silver lining in this disastrous situation. I tried to muster up the happy moments and memories during my pregnancy to get me through the night. Miraculously, after tossing and turning for countless hours, my mind finally stopped racing, settled and allowed me to get some much-needed rest for the journey ahead.

### *The Hospital*

On our way to the hospital I was an emotional wreck. I cried the entire ten-minute ride to the hospital because I felt like I was on my way to a funeral. I couldn't help but think…WHY ME? WHY MY BABY? WHY MY FAMILY? WHY GIVE ME A PIECE OF HEAVEN ONLY TO SNATCH IT AWAY TWELVE WEEKS FROM THE FINISH LINE? All these things were blaring through my mind on our drive over, coupled with an endless supply of tears streaming down my face while gospel music poured into my subconscious spirit. When we got to the hospital my husband checked me in while I sat in the lobby with tear-filled eyes, completing medical forms. Fifteen minutes later, we were escorted to a large, end room on the delivery floor. A nurse helped me into my gown and comforted me in a warm, mother-like embrace as she told me everything would be alright, and that God would keep me during this situation. Oddly enough, even though tears were streaming down my face, the nurse's words calmed my spirit and allowed me to refocus on the task at hand…delivering my angel.

I arrived at the hospital at 8:30 that morning and an IV was inserted into my left arm as soon as I was settled in the hospital bed. A bombardment of shots and string of questions ensued regarding decisions two young, inexperienced parents should not have to make: *"Do you want to see your baby when he's born?" "Do you want to hold your baby (even if he is deformed or discolored)?" "Do you want to name your baby?" "What funeral home do you want to use?" "Do you want the baby buried or cremated?" "Do you want the chaplain to baptize the baby?" "Do you want to have a ceremony at the hospital with your pastor for the baby?" "Do you want a photographer to take pictures of your baby?" "Do you want us to conduct an autopsy to try to find the cause of his death?"* I felt like the rapper 50 Cent in his song "21 Questions". Now, further removed from the situation, I can joke and say, Saturday, January 16, 2016 was the day my husband and I became real adults. We were forced to make some *real adult* decisions, but one thing I'm proud of, is the fact we did it as a team. We came together to do what we thought was best for us and our son's wellbeing.

Afterwards, I was given a bevy of medications to jumpstart the labor process. During the extended wait for the medicine to take effect, my husband and I officially decided we would name our son, Derrek Jerrell Anderson Jr. We wanted to see him after he was born. We wanted an autopsy conducted to see if we could find the cause of his death. We wanted him cremated instead of buried so we could have him with us if we ever moved. And we wanted pictures taken to cherish our memories of him.

Day 1 was full of decision making and stagnate labor. My mother flew into Georgia from Michigan to be with my husband and I as our support during this tough time. At first, I didn't expect my mom to come down in a day's notice, but she insisted on being there, if not for anything else than moral support, and boy was I happy she came. Between my husband and my mother, they intercepted calls and texts from people trying to check on me. At that moment, I didn't have the energy to talk or try to explain the situation as I was still trying to wrap my own mind around all that was taking place. By the end of Day 1, I had only dilated approximately one centimeter, and I needed to get to ten.

Day 2, Sunday, January 17, 2016…was a waiting game. I waited for the second and third medicine options to kick in to speed up my induced labor, so I could deliver my baby boy. By midnight, I was starting to have very minor contractions, nothing significant enough to kickstart delivery, so I rested before awaking around 4 a.m. in pain. I had dilated to three centimeters and was given a dose of Pitocin to get the party started. After the Pitocin was administered, I started feeling major cramps, so I asked for an epidural. The nurse who administered the epidural made my husband and mom exit the room while she explained to me the procedure. Then she administered my epidural around 5:40 a.m. Within an hour of getting the epidural, I felt immense pressure in my lower abdominal region. I had my mom go retrieve my nurse. She came in, checked me and said I was going into labor. They could see my son's head crowning. She told me, after two days of labor, I was finally ready to push. I pushed three times and not even fifteen minutes later, at 6:48 a.m. on Monday, January 18, 2016 (Martin Luther King Day), my son, Derrek Jerrell Anderson Jr. "DJ", was born.

Although born a sleeping angel surrounded by complete silence, my profound love for DJ was instant. When I saw his handsome face and tiny frame at one pound, 5.30 ounces and twelve inches long, I marveled at how my son was the most beautiful baby I'd ever seen. He had long fingers (like I did when I was a baby) and huge feet (not sure where he inherited those). He had a head full of black straight hair, rosy red cheeks and lips, and a tiny button nose. Although his eyes were closed, we were able to gently lift his eyelids to get a glimpse of their chestnut brown color. After being cleaned up and swaddled in a blanket, my son was handed to me.

Initially, I wasn't sure how Derrek and I would feel when we got our first glimpse of him, but, surprisingly, we were both calm and at peace while we examined and admired the tiny creation we had made. Although he wasn't alive, I felt like a proud mommy in that very moment. I snapped pictures of him, his face, his tiny hands, and his huge feet, before passing him off to my husband. Throughout my pregnancy, Derrek had had some reservations that the baby would be too small and fragile for him to hold. But he held our baby like a pro. During our time together, I examined every crevice, curve, and inch of his warm, lifeless body. I was staring at a real-life angel and was in awe of the indelible impression this tiny human being would leave on my heart. As my husband and I gushed over our tiny bundle of joy, in that moment, all was right with the world. Our munchkin was out, safe, in good hands, had no outer deformities, and looked normal on initial examination after being born twelve weeks early. Do I wish I could've held my baby on April 7th ALIVE, HEALTHY, and BREATHING? Of course, but I tried to make the best of the situation. I tried to take my lemons and make lemonade.

After an hour of us spending time together as a family, our nurse came and retrieved DJ to weigh him, measure him, take his fingerprints and footprints, and capture a lock of his hair, for our keepsake box. During the time our son was being cared for by the nursing staff, my husband and I selected a funeral home and signed a death certificate. Later, we were presented with a box full of mementos to remember our son, which included: blankets, hats, books, ornaments, a feather, a charm, a christening outfit, resources, and a teddy bear. We also had our son's pictures taken, which turned out to be the second-best decision we made that day, the first being the decision to see him, hold him, and spend precious time with him after he was born.

When the nurses finished with him, they returned him back to us, so we could spend our last time together as a trio. We shared quiet moments as a family, creating precious memories that I will never forget. Once the photographer came into the room and took pictures of DJ with us, his footprints and handprints were documented, and we said our eternal goodbyes for the final time. That was the hardest thing we had to do that day. We held DJ one last time. We kissed him, hugged him, prayed for him, and dedicated him back to Christ where he could dwell amongst our heavenly father and the other angels in peace. I apologized to him for not being able to provide him with the necessary things to keep him safe, then we thanked him for choosing us to be his parents. When we finished our prayer, we gave him one final round of hugs and kisses and sadly placed him in a tiny bed where he was rolled away for good. That was such a bittersweet moment. In the words of Nicki Minaj, "I wish that I could have that moment for life." Afterwards, my husband and I sat in silence while tears streamed down our faces, repeatedly replaying the encounter we had with an angel.

### Packing Up

Once we said our goodbyes to DJ, I was encouraged to walk around the hospital delivery wing to help feeling return to my legs after receiving the epidural. I was able to do several laps of the delivery wing without assistance fairly easy but very cautiously. My mom was walking by my side and marveled at how strong I had been throughout the entire ordeal from showing up to the hospital, being in labor, delivering DJ, and making a host of tough decisions. In that very moment, I was like a kid gushing at the fact that I made my parent proud. It wasn't something I intended to do in the moment. I was just doing what was required of me as DJ's mom, but it did make me feel good to know that my mom thought I, along with my husband, were doing a great job at playing the cards we were dealt as new parents ourselves.

During the hours following the birth of DJ and me getting discharged from the hospital, I spoke with my doctor about the next steps in my recovery. I also had an in-depth conversation with my nurse Ginger, who explained what to expect from those around me after being discharged and the grief process in general following a stillbirth. Amid our heart-to-heart conversation, Nurse Ginger told me that grieving for a lost child would be an unpredictable journey. She explained to me that some days would be great, but others would be very tough. She told me not to get down on myself if I cried and cried and cried over the loss of someone I created in my own womb. She also mentioned that people could possibly distance themselves from me because they have no idea what to say and it can make them feel very uncomfortable discussing the death of a baby.

On the flip side, she warned me about good-intentioned people who mean well, but in their attempt to comfort me, may say things that will offend me. Another thing she mentioned, was the fact that I may even stumble into depression because the weight of the loss could be so heavy on me. She also made it a point to encourage me not to be afraid to reach out and ask for help from my spouse, parents, siblings, friends, church members or even a therapist or support group if I needed it.

On top of all the solid advice nurse Ginger offered, she even provided me with literature for not only myself but for my husband, and our parents on how to cope with loss as grandparents. According to both our parents, the information helped tremendously. I was also given a list of resources and digital support groups I could reach out to for help with jumpstarting my grief journey.

The last and most important thing we discussed before we parted ways was the fact that my husband and I would grieve differently. Nurse Ginger encouraged Derrek and I to simply lean on each other and God when times were tough, and to remember that better days were ahead. That advice was the soundest advice I received throughout my stay. I was so thankful for her candid advice because she gave me a glimpse of what life could look like once I escaped the hospital bubble of comfort, support, and the proper knowledge about stillborn experiences.

Between my doctor, Doctor Thomas, and my nurse, Ginger, those two were godsends. They eased my fears at every step of the process and prepared me for the long journey ahead. They answered any questions I had no matter how miniscule they might have seemed which set my mother, husband, and myself at ease. My stay at the hospital let me know that God had truly listened to my prayers when I had asked Him for peace two nights prior. He provided me with the most loving hospital staff I could find. They were very attentive, careful with me, understanding, in-tune with my feelings and emotions, and just truly took care of me in my most vulnerable state.

I cannot stress enough how important it is to find a team of people (especially when you are dealing with stillbirth) who are sympathetic to your situation and truly want the best for you. It makes a world of difference. I've heard horror stories from mom's in support groups who weren't shown the same level of compassion or understanding that I experienced during my stay at the hospital and how different their stillbirth experiences turned out because of it. If there is anything I can say that is a must as a stillbirth parent, it would be to go into the hospital prepared with a list of needs you would like to have met to send your baby off exactly how you want.

If you want to see your baby, request it. If you want to hold your baby, make that known. If you want a photographer to come in and capture your baby's photos don't be afraid to do that. If you want to bathe your baby or dress him or her go for it. These moments are once in a lifetime. You will never get this time back. There are no do-overs, so you have to get it right the first time around. Even though I went in blindly, I'm glad my nursing staff asked all the right questions (even though at the time they seemed overwhelming) to make my experience one-of-a-kind.

As I began to pack my belongings to leave the hospital, I felt like a soldier returning home from war. It was an experience that most would not face in their lifetimes. There was a newly formulated bond with my husband. We had been through so much in the course of three days that not many could say they endured. I was so proud of how we came together as a unit to make life-changing decisions for our son. I thought we made it through the worst part of the storm, but truly, the grief process was just beginning. In the hospital, I was in my own small bubble of comfort, reasoning, and understanding. However, the real-world was awaiting me. I said my final goodbyes to my doctor, nursing staff, and to DJ before I was placed in a wheel chair and rolled out of the hospital (the same day I delivered my sleeping angel), empty-handed!

*You left your footprints on our hearts!*

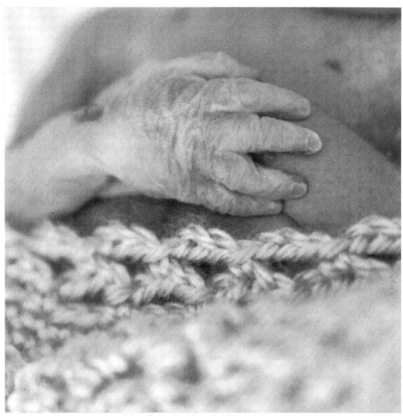

*The hands that hold my heart*

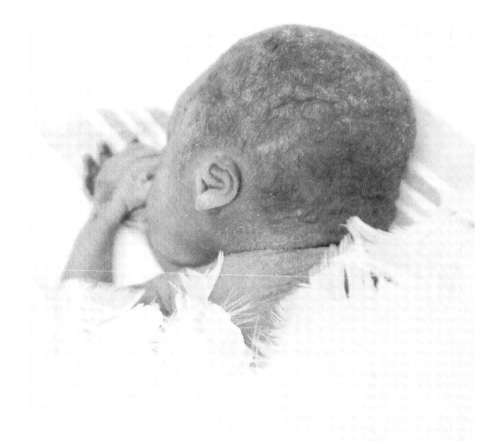

*You're our angel!*

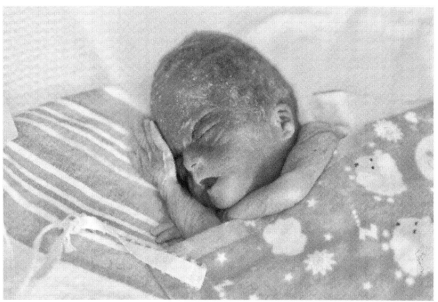

*My sleeping angel, just as peaceful as can be.*

# Chapter 3

## What To Expect At The Hospital

*"Be on guard. Stand firm in the faith.*
*Be courageous. Be strong."*
*– 1 Corinthians 16:13, New Living Translation*

When I was admitted to the hospital to begin inducing my labor, I was like a fish out of water. I really didn't know what to do when I got there because I had never been admitted to a hospital prior to this incident. Of course, I've been to the doctor's office for checkups, but I never had something so severe happen to me where a trip to the hospital was warranted. When we arrived at the hospital, my husband checked me in at the front desk because I was an emotional wreck. After filling out all the paper work, through a veil of tears, we were escorted to a large private room at the end of the hall on the delivery ward. I wasn't sure how I would handle being in a wing where other women were delivering healthy babies they would take home, but surprisingly, the experience ended up being a good one. Well, as good as it could be for going in to deliver your deceased child.

In the room, I changed into a hospital gown and was given an IV. Afterwards, I was informed that a host of nurses and medical professionals would be coming in and out of the room throughout the course of the day to check on me and run various labs. If you're afraid of needles, now is the time to get a hold of your fear because you will be poked and pricked a lot during your stay. One thing I truly respected and appreciated with the hospital, was the fact they placed a card outside the door with a fallen leaf to represent a mother experiencing miscarriage, stillbirth, or infant loss. The simple gesture was a way to notify healthcare professionals prior to entering your room to be a bit more sensitive with the questions they asked you and how they interacted with you. At first, I didn't think this was such a big deal, but the sensitivity made a world of a difference when it got closer and closer to the point I had to deliver DJ.

After the initial shock of being told you will have to deliver your stillborn baby, your memory can get a little hazy as you try your best to mentally prepare for your hospital stay. To be fully prepped for your sleeping angel's delivery I compiled a list of tips that I wished I was privy to prior to my three-day hospital stay.

**Tip #1 for grieving parents: Have predetermined answers to questions the doctor's or nursing staff may ask you.**

Prior to even going to the hospital I would make sure that you had a general idea of what your response to those tough questions will be, so you're not caught off guard like we were. I know this may seem like a daunting task, especially after having your world crashed down around you, but I think it is a good idea to be prepared and have your answers mapped out in your head so when you get to the hospital, all your bases are covered.

**Tip #2 for grieving parents: Make sure you are on the same page with your partner.**

It is imperative that you and your partner are on one accord when it comes to making decisions that will impact you for years to come. Even if the idea of something may scare either of you at the time, it may be worth doing anyway because you only get one shot to experience your baby in the flesh after losing them through stillbirth. Be sure to honestly consult with your partner to see what you both want from this disheartening process.

**Tip #3 for grieving parents: Consider whether you will want to see your baby and how you will capture your baby's memory.**

At first, when I envisioned seeing my lifeless child in my arms, I thought it would make me sad. I wasn't sure I wanted to see him prior to my trip to the hospital. However, after texting one of my closest friends, Gyreasha, the day before we were scheduled to go into the hospital, she recommended that I consider seeing DJ. She explained to me that her cousin had been through a similar stillbirth experience with one of her children, and while it was difficult at first to think of the thought of holding her deceased baby, it was one of the best decisions she made. She said being able to meet and finally see the tiny human that was growing inside her helped her tremendously with closure.

With her wave of confidence and after searching for pictures on the internet of stillborn babies, I decided, with the help of my husband, that I too would see my son when he was born no matter how he looked. I cannot decide what is best for you and your situation, but, if you have the option, I highly recommend you electing to not only see your child/children but to also hold them and spend time with them (if your healthcare staff deems it possible). The quiet time you get to spend as a family can be very therapeutic. It can also assist with closure and help minimize any regrets you may have. If you don't physically want to see your baby, I would, at a minimum, suggest you get your child's pictures taken. Even if you don't look at the pictures immediately, you can have them tucked away to look at when you are ready, so you can at least have an idea of what your child looked like in their angelic glory.

**Tip #4 for grieving parents: Eat a well-balanced meal before being admitted to the hospital (unless advised otherwise by your healthcare providers).**

You will get to eat food at the beginning stages of your labor after being induced, but once the contractions get to two to three centimeters apart, you are no longer allowed to eat until after you have delivered your baby, regardless of how long it takes. Eating something hearty before going into the hospital will help tie you over until your next good meal, unless otherwise advised by your medical staff. Once I was restricted from eating, all I was permitted to consume was water, grape juice, ice, and chicken broth from Sunday to Monday morning. I had worked up a huge appetite by the time my son arrived, so keep this in mind.

**Tip #5 for grieving parents: Pack an overnight bag like you are going into delivery.**

Don't forget to pack your overnight bag. When we first spoke with our doctor, she made inducing my labor seem like a quick outpatient type of procedure. She said they would induce me, then I would have the baby. The way she explained it, my husband and I thought I would be at the hospital no longer than three or four hours max. What a naive mindset. Instead of being admitted into the hospital for three hours we were there for three days. I didn't pack anything but my iPad, iPhone and their respective chargers. Just like you would pack an overnight bag when you are going to deliver a healthy baby, you need to do the same for your sleeping angel. Here are some items you may want to include in your overnight bag:

- A picture ID (driver's license or other form of ID)
- Your insurance cards
- Any paperwork given to you by your doctor to bring to the hospital
- Any questions you may have for the hospital staff caring for you during your stay
- Eyeglasses and your contacts (if you wear them) along with your contact case, glasses case, and contact solution (if you have 20/20 vision and don't need the assistance of glasses or contact solution count your blessings)
- A bathrobe

- A nightgown or two (you are provided with a gown at the hospital but if you prefer your own you may be allowed to wear it after speaking with your nursing staff)
- Slippers or slides to walk around your room and/or the hospital
- Socks (with grips at the bottom) it sometimes gets really cold in the room. All you're wearing is a gown, so it's good to have something to put on your feet
- Things that can help you relax
  - Pillow
  - Blanket
  - Music on your phone
  - Tablet, Phone, Coloring book, cards etc. (anything to help pass the time away)
- A camera or video camera (if you want to document your sleeping angel's delivery or chronicle your own photos of your baby after he or she is born)
- Batteries, chargers, and memory cards for your [video] camera
- Toiletries
  - Toothbrush
  - Toothpaste
  - Deodorant
  - Soap or Body Wash
  - Shower Shoes
  - Lotion
  - Floss
  - Mouth Wash
  - Shampoo
  - Conditioner
  - Facial Cleanser

- o   Wash cloth (the hospital will provide you with one if you don't have it)
- o   Towel (the hospital will provide you with one if you don't have it)
- o   Lip balm
- o   Brush
- o   Comb
- o   Makeup (optional)
- o   Heavy-flow sanitary napkins
- Snacks
  - o   Crackers
  - o   Fresh or dried fruit
  - o   Granola bars
  - o   Anything you think you will enjoy (before you can no longer partake in eating anything)
- Something to read or watch
- Cell phone
- Cell phone charger
- Comfortable bra/Sports bra (after giving birth your milk may come in, which will cause your breast to feel tender, use a tight sports bra to help ease some of the discomfort)
- Maternity underwear (the hospital will provide you with a handful of mesh underwear as well as sanitary pads because you may bleed after delivery, but you can opt to use your own undergarments if you feel more comfortable by doing so)
- Notepad and pen/pencil to take down notes, contact information of the staff (names, number, email etc.), jot down any important information
- An outfit to go home in (something easy to slip into), a pair of flat comfortable shoes

- You may want to bring some thank you cards to address to your nursing staff and doctor (only if they do an exceptional job with your care...my nursing staff did an amazing job, one in particular whom I connected with, Ginger...I didn't bring thank you cards with me so I got her business card and sent her a thank you card just to say thanks for her support, kindness, gentleness, and attentiveness in our roughest, darkest hour)
- Items for your sleeping angel (optional): You may want to bring items to use during your bonding time with your sleeping angel. This is totally optional, but handy to know just in case you are interested in these bonding activities before saying your final goodbyes to your angel.
    - Towels, Shampoo, Baby Body Wash in case you want to give your baby a bath (if your medical staff allows you to bathe your baby)
    - An outfit for your sleeping angel, if you want him/her to wear something other than what the hospital provides for the pictures they may take (if you so choose)
    - Comb and/or brush if you want to comb/brush your babies hair

During our stay, my husband went back home and gathered up some items, I would need since our three-hour stay turned into a three-day adventure. Thankfully, we stayed less than fifteen minutes away from the hospital. Although I came to the hospital with nothing besides my purse, my phone, and iPad, I left with some amazing keepsakes donated by local organizations:

- Memory book with my son's birth information, nursing staff information, doctor's information, hand and footprints
- Receiving blanket with a scripture tag attached to it. My son was wrapped in the blanket when he was born. Although it had blood splatters on it, we opted to keep it to remind us of him
- A crocheted turquoise baby blanket with a matching hat
- A rainbow colored crocheted baby blanket
- A keepsake box with a butterfly on the front
- Official hospital wristbands with our son's name and birthdate on it
- A teddy bear
- A translucent Christmas ornament with a feather and blue glitter inside. A note was attached that said, "A feather from an angel is one we hardly see. But this one is quite different, and as special as can be. This feather is a reminder of a special person's love…who is now a guardian angel, watching from above."
- Small cloth diaper with a safety pin (made from fabric that says little buddy on the backside)
- A white feather with a gold-dipped tip along with an attached card that said, "Feathers appear when angels are near."
- Paper ruler with my son's weight, length, and birthdate on it (it was the ruler our nurse used to measure DJ)
- Three silver pendants (an angel wing, heart, and baby footprints) to attach to a charm bracelet
- A small plastic box with a few locks of my son's hair
- A candle

- A christening outfit for a baby boy
- A book entitled Still by Stephanie Paige Cole (a wonderful one day read that helped me the day I returned home from the hospital)
- A folder from the hospital that included patient information, post-partum instructions, and other miscellaneous paperwork
- A grief folder which included:
  - DJ's Identification Card
  - Certificate of Birth with his handprints and footprints on the back
  - Recognition Certificate of Life with his footprints, name, date of birth, time of birth, weight, length, and parent names
  - Newborn Identification Paper with my information, my finger print, my son's footprints, his sex, date of birth, race, weight, length, doctor and nurse's signature
  - Funeral home information (all which was free of charge for parents experiencing baby loss, at my particular hospital)
  - Discharge instructions after losing a baby
  - A card they put on my door so medical staff would know I was a stillbirth patient
  - A card with a morning prayer
  - Information about grief groups I could join digitally or in person in surrounding areas
  - A coupon for fifteen percent off at Little Winged Ones, a company that creates memorial sketches of babies lost to stillbirth or infant death

o   Information about stillbirth, autopsy, a mother's grief, a father's grief, and even grandparent's grief

As you can see, my hospital gifted me with some amazing keepsakes to commemorate the loss of my son. While I would have loved to have taken home a healthy bouncing baby, these thoughtful mementos truly eased the pain I felt leaving empty handed. Although we had a professional photographer take some beautiful photographs of our son, I still elected to snap my own pictures with my iPhone when our nurse gave us the chance to have some private time with DJ. Between the pictures I took, and those complimentary images provided by our awesome photographer, I stored them on my phone and looked at those pictures multiple times a day. I still look at the pictures of my son daily. They bring me such joy and comfort to know that I had a part (along with my husband) in creating an angel. As soon as I saw his face, a wave of pride rushed over me. I could not believe I created someone so amazing. Even lifeless in my arms, he was the most handsome baby I had ever seen. He looked a lot like my husband.

I'm saying all this to say that your stay at the hospital is what you make it. I went in feeling very emotional and slightly defeated, but I left feeling strong and empowered, knowing I had just birthed a real-life angel. My only advice to offer you during your hospital stay is take as much control of the situation that you can and do what makes sense for you and your partner. If you want to see your baby and hold your baby, do so. If you want to plan a memorial service and bury your child, do that! Whatever makes you happy and gives you the most closure, do it. You were assigned the task of being the parent(s) of a special sleeping angel. This mission is not given to the faint of heart. While the hospital is the first stop on the grief train, just know that the journey you have ahead is one to prep for.

# Chapter 4

## The Never Ending Why

*"Cast all your anxiety on Him,*
*because He cares for you."*
*– **1 Peter 5:7**, New American Standard Bible*

So many things were flowing through my head.

- Why you?

- Why me?

- Why us?

- Why do some babies live?

- Why do some babies die?

- Why couldn't they save you at twenty-eight weeks, when they save some babies far younger than you?

- What didn't I do correctly?

- Did I overwork myself?

- Was I stressed?

- Was I too active?

- Was I not active enough?

- Did I not show enough appreciation for you?

- Did I eat harmful foods?

- Did I not eat enough of the good stuff to help you grow?

- Was I operating in an ignorant state of bliss?

- Should I have informed the doctors sooner that I didn't feel too much movement from you earlier in my pregnancy?

- Why did I just assume you were a calm baby?

- Why didn't I voice more concerns about you and your lack of movement to the doctor?

- Why did you have to go?

- Why am I not able to hold you?

- Why is your existence dwindled to a picture in a frame?

- Why do I have to constantly bring up your name for people to remember your legacy?

- Why couldn't I make it twelve more weeks to the finish line?

- Why do I have to carry on without you?

- Why did I get inducted into a club that no parent wants to belong to?

- Why did I get robbed of the innocence and joy of pregnancy that everyone else gets to experience?

- Why do tears fall when I least expect them too?

- Why am I always crying?

- Why am I suffering in silence?

- Why won't this sadness leave?

- Why can't I see your handsome face?

- Why aren't you here with me?

- Why did we have to experience this pain?

- Why is grief a never-ending destination?

- Why do we have to see others basking in the joys of parenthood while we sit idly by heartbroken?

- Why do I have to start all over again (I had a perfectly healthy baby)?

- Why couldn't the doctors tell me what caused your death?

- Why am I writing this sad screen play (I should be holding you in my arms witnessing the awesome human you get to become daily)?

- Why do I only have *things* to remind me of you, instead of *you* being here with me?

- Why do I feel so empty inside?

- Why do I only get to see you in my thoughts and dreams?

- Why didn't I ever get to experience your cry? Your laugh? Your curiosity? Your love? Your dependence on me and your daddy? Your intelligence?

- Why can't I ever change your diaper?

- Why can't I observe you take your first steps or hear you say your first words?

- Why can't I teach you right from wrong?

- Why can't I witness your amazing personality?

- Why can't I see you grow into a cool human being?

- Why do I have to talk to a tiny urn to feel you near?

- Why did you get snatched away from me with no warning?

- Why did my body fail you?

- Why does it feel like I got hit by a ton of bricks?

- Why can't I explain how I feel?

- Why did I have to celebrate my first Mother's Day without you?

- Why did people expect me to go "back to normal" after we loss you?

- What is normal?

- Why do I have to ask all these questions?

- Why did the best thing that ever happened to me (besides marrying your dad) get snatched away from me?

- Why did my excitement turn into a nightmare overnight, in the blink of an eye?

- Why didn't I do more for you?

- Why do I have stretch marks reminding me daily of your existence, but no baby to show for them?

- Why did I gain so much weight when I only had a one-pound baby inside me?

- Why didn't I do more to save you?

- Why do I get sad when I see other women with baby bumps?

- Why do pregnancy commercials hurt me?

- Why did I burst into tears when I saw a woman changing her newborn in the bathroom stall at a restaurant?

- Why did you lose your life?

- Why can't we turn back the hands of time and rewrite all our wrongs?

- Why does life deal us such sucky hands?

- Why did we have to call our families and explain you were no longer with us?

- How am I supposed to go on without you?

- Why does it feel like there is a void I will never be able to fill?

- Why do people think if I have another baby it will erase all the pain I feel with losing you?

- Why do people think another baby will heal the wounds?

- Why do people think another baby will solve the problem of your absence?

- Why do people say cliché things like *"it was all in God's plan?"*

- What lesson is God trying to teach me?

- Am I failing or passing the test God has thrown my way?

- Will there be a testimony at the end of this tragedy (I sure hope so)?

- Why did I have to avoid going to church on Mother's Day?

- Why did I spend my thirtieth birthday running away from the true pain I felt losing you a few weeks prior?

- Why does my husband (your daddy) have to hold me at night because I can't stop crying?

- Why did God make a way for other babies but not for mine?

- Why am I here?

- Why do I have to celebrate the life of a new niece or nephew while I have to mourn the life of my son?

- How am I supposed to remain happy when sadness is deep-rooted beneath the surface?

- Why do I try to hold it all together when some days I just wish I could punch a wall and scream?

- Why do I have to start over again? Seriously, why?

- Why don't doctors inform us more about the dark side of pregnancy (miscarriage, stillbirth, infant loss)?

- Why is losing a baby such a taboo subject?

- Why do I feel like an outcast sentenced to a life of isolation?

- Why is it, whenever I see a baby that is the same age you should've been, I reminisce about you?

- Why do I keep track of how long it's been since I last saw your face?

- Why do I still have pregnancy apps on my phone tracking your due date?

- Why did I have to say hello and goodbye on the same day?

- Why do I have to figure out how to keep your legacy and name relevant?

- Why don't more people ask about you?

- Why do I feel like I have to continuously bring you up to get people to notice you were truly here?

- Why do I experience such highs and lows?

- Why doesn't grief have an expiration date?

- How do I make sure I never forget you?

- Where do I go from here?

- Why do I feel like a failure when it comes to you?

- Why do all these questions still exist in my head five months after you left this earth?

- Will it ever get better, fully?

- What does better even look like?

- Why didn't I get my happy ending?

- Why do I feel like I'm living in a bad dream that I can't wake up from?

- Why do I pull out the onesies and clothing I bought for you and blankly stare at them, thinking of what could have been?

- Why do we still have boxes of unopened diapers in the closet?

- Why do I wonder what life would be like with you here?

- Why am I constantly fighting to see the bright side in this dull situation?

- What is the point of being an optimist?

- Why do I want to rewind time back to January 15, 2016 so I can get a do over of your last ultrasound?

- Why did I have to hear that you had no heartbeat?

- Why didn't I record the sound of your heart when I first heard it on the fetal Doppler?

- Why didn't I take progressive bump pictures each month to chronicle our brief time spent together?

- Why did I make my pregnancy so public only to be humiliated publicly by your loss?

- Why do you sometimes feel like a distant memory that I don't want to let go of?

- Why does it sometimes seem like you were just a dream I imagined in another life?

- Did you pass away peacefully or were you in pain?

- Did you hear us (me and daddy) talk to you and pray for you every night?

- Did you know your dad knew you were a boy the day I got pregnant and that he already picked your name out way before you were born or conceived?

- Did you know I felt like a total let down to your dad because he was so excited to name you after him?

- Did you know I blame myself for your death?

- Why did I have to make a playlist of songs to draw me closer to you when I didn't have the right words to say?

- Why did I play Lailah Hathaway's rendition of Anita Baker's song Angel to you every day? Was it a glimpse into the future? Were you preparing me for not being here with me?

- How is heaven?

- Do you miss us like we miss you?

- Do you get to sit at the feet of Jesus?

- Did you meet other [stillbirth, miscarriage, or infant loss] angels?

- Do you have friends?

- Do you think about us?

These are just a portion of questions that crossed my mind at some point during my grief journey. Questions I have stored in my subconscious. Questions that don't really have resolutions but ones I pondered religiously for an answer. At any given moment, these questions can float into my mind and instantly alter my mood or draw up emotions that are not necessarily conducive to my well-being or happiness. So, why do these questions even exist? Why do they fester in my mind when I know there is no end game in sight? I'm not sure there is really an answer. But one thing I was told by my therapist, Dr. Holly Brown, is that it is okay to have questions. It is okay to sift through countless scenarios of the "what if" game. She assured me that the questioning process is often a small piece of the grief puzzle.

I know many of you have probably pondered these same questions or encountered similar variations of questions provided on this list. You may even have a plethora of other questions you could add to this endless rabbit-hole of questioning. Just know that asking questions or trying to figure out what happened to cause your loss is neither silly, dumb, or crazy; it simply makes us more human...dealing with the raw emotions that come along with grief and loss.

My therapist once told me it's a good habit to dump all your why's and thoughts on paper. She said it's good practice to release the emotions that come with them, and once they are out to try not to linger on them for too long. She suggested setting a specific time limit (five minutes, ten minutes, thirty minutes, one hour etc.) to get all your questions out and come up with suitable answers then to let them go once you've found satisfactory answers to help you "move on." She reminded me often in our sessions that it's not a good idea to dwell on the why's because no matter what, you can't change the outcome of what happened. You just have to try to pick up the shattered pieces as best as you can and do your best to live in a state of gratitude (even on your darkest days).

### *Things to Keep in Mind When Questioning Your Loss*

1.  There are many questions that will pop into your mind on a daily basis that will attempt to seek out why you had to experience stillbirth or any other type of pregnancy loss.

2.  Know that it is okay to acknowledge the questions you have. Remember it is perfectly fine to dump your questions from your subconscious. There are no bad questions as long as you acknowledge they are there.

3.  Do not harp on these questions day after day, night after night. Give yourself a time limit to purge your questions and get them out of your system then prepare to move forward in some type of productive way.

4.  If it helps, answer your questions using a reply that is satisfactory to your healing. It may not be the truth but if it helps you cope with your loss, use your made-up reply as a response to your revolving door of never ending whys. Who knows, you may even land on the truth through

your relentless discovery of sifting through your whys.

# Chapter 5

## Emotions

*"And now, dear brothers and sisters, one final thing.*
*Fix your thoughts on what is true, and honorable,*
*and right, and pure, and lovely, and admirable.*
*Think about things that are excellent and worthy of*
*praise."*
**– Philippians 4:8** *New Living Translation*

You may experience a gamut of emotions throughout the various stages of your grief journey. It's funny how you can wake up perfectly fine, and without any rhyme or reason, something can "trigger" your emotions. These triggers can derail your entire day if you allow them. The emotions you experience can range from feeling on top of the world to the world crashing down on you in a matter of minutes. In this chapter, we will discuss some of the emotions you may be faced with and how to handle them when they arise.

As mentioned previously there are a ton of emotions that can creep in after the loss of your child. Some you may welcome openly, while others you may want to rid yourself of immediately. Like grief, emotions can be very fluid. They can fluctuate back and forth. They are not good or bad, they just are. The way to move past certain emotions is to first acknowledge that they are there; let them occur, then pick yourself up and go forth. Here are some typical emotions you may encounter after losing your child:

- Love

- Admiration

- Sadness

- Gratitude

- Thankfulness

- Anger

- Jealousy

- Envy

- Hope

- Stress

- Pressure

- Disappointment

- Confusion

- Happiness

- Peace

- Rage

- Depression

- Madness

- Anguish

- Anxiety

- Empathy

- An "I Don't Care" Attitude

- Worthlessness

- Empty

These are just a handful of many emotions you may experience after the loss of your angel. There are a few emotions I want to harp on that challenged me often, especially at the beginning of my never-ending grief journey. The main emotions that seem to be on a continuous spin cycle for me are gratitude or thankfulness, peace, sadness, disappointment, jealousy/envy, and emptiness. As stated earlier, grief is very individualized. If these are not the emotions you deal with on a regular basis, that doesn't make your grief process wrong; it simply means you grieve differently, and that is okay!

### *Gratitude/Thankfulness*

When I initially think about my son, the first emotion that usually presents itself is gratitude or thankfulness. I am grateful for the time I got to spend with DJ. We created a special bond for twenty-eight amazing weeks. I always said he was such a sweet baby because I never once had morning sickness. I didn't have trouble keeping food down. I didn't get nauseated, I didn't experience headaches, or any other uncomfortable symptoms new mommies typically experience during their first trimester. The only thing I experienced with my first few weeks of pregnancy with DJ was fatigue. I was always tired. It's pretty taxing creating a life inside of you. I am grateful for the quiet moments DJ and I shared, when I sang to him, read to him, imagined who he would look like and what type of personality he would have. My favorite moments had been when my husband and I laid down for the night and we prayed as a family for the safe arrival of our little munchkin. Memories like these fill my gratefulness meter daily and allow me to view this tragic situation with a "glass half full" mentality. While I cannot sit here and say I am always in a state of thankfulness, I try to revert to this state the most, because I truly do believe that Derrek Jr. was one of the biggest blessings in my life to date.

### *Peace*

Another emotion or state of being I find myself often in, is a state of peace. While by no means am I fine with how things ended with DJ, I know there isn't anything I could do differently to bring him back physically. I try to operate in a state of peace for my own sanity. I will never forget when I first found out that DJ transitioned into an angel. I came home and prayed. I knew I had a tough task ahead of me with the responsibility of delivering this tiny blessing. So, I prayed mightily for peace. I asked God to grant me a sense of peace to face the insurmountable challenge of delivering my deceased son. Other than my tear-filled entrance into the hospital, I felt an immediate overwhelming sense of peace. It was like God was there propping me up on both sides during my lowest moment. I felt a huge sense of calm, purpose, and an unshakable belief that everything would be okay during my stay at Houston (pronounced House – ton) Medical Center. If you've never experienced peace, I highly recommend you pray for peace in your situation. It can tremendously increase your faith in God, and your belief that all things can work together for your good even in the bleakest of situations. Most of all it can offer your mind a tranquility like no other, even if the pieces around you are shattered.

### Deep Sadness

While gratitude, thankfulness, and peace are amazing spaces to dwell after a tragic loss, there are some emotions that will come around that aren't so pleasant. One of those emotions is deep sadness or sorrow. This emotion was typically accompanied by an endless stream of tears in my case. This sadness is like a passenger nestled deep within. It doesn't need a cause, it simply swells up like the ocean tides. This deep sadness never really goes away; you are just able to control it better as time goes on.

When DJ first passed away, I was constantly in tears for hours at a time. Most nights I would just cry myself to sleep because that was all I could do. I wouldn't even use tissue because I could go through entire rolls, wiping away my surge of steady tears. I would keep a small face towel draped across the top of the headrest of my bed to dry the stream of tears that were guaranteed to show up at some point during the night. I would awake with red eyes, a tear-stained pillow case, and a pit of sadness. Then slowly, but surely, the tears stopped occurring every day and made their appearance every other day, then once a week. Now, the tears fall more sporadically. I can't say every day has sunny skies, but it has gotten much better. I urge you to extend yourself grace during your moments of sadness and allow yourself time to trust your own grief process. If you feel like your tears and deep sadness have overstayed their welcome for far too long, don't be afraid to seek help from wise council – be it from your pastor, spouse, or a licensed therapist.

Keep in mind your continuous state of sadness can make people around you very uncomfortable. So uncomfortable in fact, those same people may feel your grief clock has run out of time, hitting 0:00. Once they assume you've had ample amount of time to grieve they may begin to expect you to pick up the pieces and move on with your life. Remind them deep sadness is an acceptable feeling you will often experience during your time of grieving. And there is no time limit on grief, especially when it comes to losing a child, whether you've never met them, held their lifeless body in your arms, or they were stripped away after spending a short time on earth.

*Disappointment*

Occasionally, disappointment rears its head. While gratitude is the state I try to operate in most, disappointment does cross my brainwaves ever so often. The disappointment comes when I think about the what ifs. The disappointments are steeped within the fact when my son's heart stopped beating, I lost all possibilities of his future. The disappointments arise when I think about the firsts I will never get to encounter with DJ. I will never know what it's like for my son to look me in the eyes and gaze lovingly. I will never know the bond a mother and child experience during breastfeeding. I will never know what it is like to hear my baby cry, giggle, or laugh. I will never get to experience my son's smile. I will never get to see how my son takes in the sights, smells, sounds, colors, etc. of the amazing world around him. I will never get to change my son's diaper, experience my baby crawling, or witness him taking his first steps. I will never get a chance to hear my son call me "mama" or "mommy." I will never get to see my son explore and go on adventures using his child-like imagination to create worlds of make belief. I will never get to experience my son's first day of kindergarten, grade school, middle school, or high school. I will never get to drop my son off at daycare and long until the moment I can see his face again. I can never pick my son up and kiss his "ouchie" after a fall. I will never see my son fall in love or do the mother-son dance with him at his wedding. I can never cheer my son on as he graduates from college or watch him excel academically. I can never teach my son about God's love (that's something he will have to teach me as he gets to experience the Godhead in heaven right now). The last day DJ took his breath was the day that all this potential disappeared. It can be a disappointment to your psyche when you think about all the things you will miss out on that others may simply take for granted as a part of growing older.

### Anger

I sometimes get angry or upset that I had to be the one to lose my son. Why me? Why couldn't someone else go through this tragic situation instead of me. Why do I have to be the spokesperson of the grief fan club? Why am I not holding my son in my arms and instead writing a book about losing a child? There are so many why's you can come up with in your mind that play on a continuous loop if you choose to let them (refer to Chapter 4: The Never Ending Why, page 54). These why's can drum up a steady beat of anger from time to time. I do not suggest you stay in an angry place. It's not fun to be around someone who is angry all the time. However, I do feel like anger is a valid emotion you may experience more times than not during your grief journey. Just know you are not alone if you experience anger often at the beginning of your journey. Your anger may even linger or even grow the more time passes. But there is one thing you shouldn't allow anger to do, and that is to take you down such a dark path that it causes harm to yourself, to someone you love, or a stranger or animal. If you need help with your anger issues after the loss of your child, please do not be afraid to go and seek help. But also, keep in mind that anger is a normal emotion to feel during your grief journey, so there is no reason for you to feel guilty, embarrassed or apologetic if anger arises.

*Jealousy/Envy*

Here's an emotion I am ashamed to say I experience from time to time, but I want to be totally upfront with you. Grief is not always presented in a pretty package and wrapped in a bow. It is not always sunshine, rainbows, and unicorns. Sometimes in grief, you experience emotions you are not proud to even admit to yourself, let alone to others. I must admit when I scroll through my various social media platforms, and see all the happy pregnancy announcements, baby bumps, or beautiful babies plastered on my timeline, I can get jealous or envious of that mom, dad, or family who gets to partake in the joys of raising a child they've waited nine long months to meet. At times, I hate to see women who are nearing the end of their pregnancy journey more so than seeing pictures of babies because I was robbed of the end of my pregnancy experience. I sometimes get envious of moms whom I see out and about pushing a stroller without a care in the world with a newborn relying on them as their source of survival.

I even sometimes hate the fact that so many babies born prematurely, especially those born before twenty-eight weeks, survive, when my son was not even given the opportunity to fight for his life. Plain and simple, it sucks. What adds insult to injury is I must smile and be happy for those closest to me expecting little bundles of joy when I just want to shout…What about me? What about my son? Why did he have to lose his life, but your baby gets to keep theirs? All these questions and feelings rise to the surface when my jealousy and envy take control. I'm not going to sit here and tell you, you shouldn't experience any type of jealousy or envy because that would be hypocritical. But I will say that it is best to try to operate most from a heart of gratefulness versus a heart of hate, jealousy, and envy. I'm a work in progress, so somedays it is easier said than done. But I wanted to remind you that just because you may get jealous when you see other women happily carrying their babies, while you silently long for yours, does not make you a bad person. It simply makes you human. Don't beat yourself up. You overcame something that most cannot even fathom. Extend yourself some grace and don't be afraid to take the good along with the bad...and sometimes the downright ugly!

### *Emptiness*

It amazes me how empty our home and our hearts feel without DJ woven into the fabric of our everyday lives, since we never officially lived as a trio. We never got the chance to set up the nursery or fully rearrange our lives for our soon-to-arrive son, yet it feels like someone is missing in our family's equation. Suddenly a family of two seems incomplete, even though it has always been just Derrek and me. I often find myself wondering what DJ would be doing at various moments throughout the day. I constantly reflect how different life would be if he were here. I pull out his clothes frequently and touch them or stare at them because I long for his presence.

The emptiness sometimes isolates me because I feel no one truly understands the feeling of losing someone you longed to meet for so long. It's amazing how just seeing two lines or a plus sign on a pregnancy test can alter the feelings of who you are. You exchange your name for the title mommy as soon as it is confirmed that you are indeed pregnant. You begin to operate like a mom: preparing, nurturing, sheltering, and loving the tiny human being you are incubating. When it is all stripped away so suddenly, you feel a piece of your heart escape with the life of your little angel.

Emptiness is common, but you don't have to conquer it on your own. Nothing or no one can ever fill the void of the child you lost, however you can request love and support to help ease the pain of emptiness from your spouse, partner, loved ones, or friends. You don't have to go about this journey isolated and alone. No matter how difficult it is to discuss or explain how you are feeling don't stop trying. You shouldn't have to lose your child then experience the devastation of picking up the pieces of your shattered life alone.

With all these emotions running rampant throughout your grief journey don't try to fight them. Let them have their place and time in your life. Allow yourself to feel what you are truly feeling. You don't have to be perfect. People are watching you. They want to see how you pick up the pieces. The thing I've found most rewarding is during those days when I have it the toughest, I share with my family, friends, or even my network of followers via social media. When I share these candid, raw human emotions, those are the days I get comments about my strength, because I am willing to show the vulnerability that comes along with losing a child. I allow myself to feel the various emotions that accompany the loss of a child. I give myself slack when I feel like "I can't go on" in that moment. I allow myself the place to cry or get angry. I don't try to suppress my feelings in fear of how it will make me look or based off how people perceive me. I simply let the emotions take over me because I know they will not last always. Give yourself room to experience all sides of grief. When you look back, you will be surprised at how far you've come when it's all said and done.

# Chapter 6

## Ask And It Shall (Or Shall Not) Be Given

*"⁷Ask, and it will be given to you; seek, and you will find; knock, and it will be opened to you. ⁸ For everyone who asks receives, and he who seeks finds, and to him who knocks it will be opened."*
*– **Matthew 7:7-8** New American Standard Bible*

There is no manual or instruction that comes attached to losing your child. It is a hands-on learning experience. Although there are countless families who have been given tickets aboard the child-loss train, no experience is identical. It is one of those things where you hope it doesn't happen to you, but when it does you have to cope with it the best way you can. While some throw themselves into work or make it a sport to keep busy to stop them from thinking about the tragic experience they have encountered, others cannot seem to gain their footing, as they feel themselves slipping into an endless hole of darkness, despair, depression etc. Others try to find the bright side in the tough situation they are facing and use it to channel their pain for the good of others. None of these scenarios are right or wrong. There is no "one size fits all" approach when it comes to losing your child. This is a child you created, grew, and nurtured inside of you. That is why it is important to understand the fragility that comes along with birthing a sleeping angel.

As a grieving parent, it is important to find your voice. It is important to be honest with yourself, your spouse, your family, your friends, your other children, your job (i.e. your boss, your coworkers etc.), and even people associated with you via religious arenas and/or extracurricular activities. It is important to note that what you've considered to be your "normal life" is no longer in play. You will never go back to how things used to be prior to finding out you would be the parent of a sleeping angel. The quicker you accept this truth, the easier it will be to begin healing. During this time, you must let it be known where you are emotionally, spiritually, and psychologically, so people can understand how to best serve your needs. If you never speak up, it will be hard for people to assist you, your growth, and your progress.

You may be involved in a lot of activities outside of the home. During the time, I lost my son I was a full-time college student completing my senior year work load, I was also the President of a fashion organization, the Vice President of a Leadership Honors Society, a tutor with my church's tutoring ministry, a middle and high school ministry leader for a group of girls, as well as a member of my church's praise team. Not to mention me being a wife, a daughter, a granddaughter, a sister, an aunt, a niece, a friend etc. With all this stuff going on, I had to take a step back and truly evaluate what I needed at that given moment. After discussing with my husband,

I decided to relieve myself of some of my duties because I didn't feel like I could serve effectively in the emotional state I was in at the time.

It may be hard to sit yourself down and give yourself an "adult time out" but it may be necessary for your true healing process to begin. I had to sit down and talk with my professors, my classmates/project mates, board members, and ministry leaders to truly express I needed some "me" time to help me sort out the feelings I was experiencing, to build myself back up mentally, and to truly give myself some time to grieve. I'm used to being a busy bee, so it wasn't easy taking a load off, but it was an extremely necessary piece of the puzzle to allow me to start the healing process. Taking some time off allowed me to truly be in touch with what I was feeling and helped me to begin to heal without all the outside distractions.

If you're used to pleasing others or not used to truly expressing what you need, this may be a difficult step in your grieving journey. After a few counseling sessions, my therapists told me that I needed to speak up and let the people around me know what I needed. If something bothers you…be honest. You will probably be put in some situations where you must speak up because someone will say or do something to you regarding your loss that will upset you, sadden you, or simply offend you. Nine out of ten times, the people that offend you have no idea that their actions or words are causing you turmoil and it usually will come from someone you're close to. That is why it is necessary to find your voice, so that the behaviors that make you cringe can be eliminated quickly.

### The Tattoo

I wanted to do something to honor my son's memory. I pondered and pondered and decided that I would get a tattoo to honor his legacy and short time spent on this earth. I wanted to get the tattoo on the one-month anniversary of his loss, February 18, 2016. Unfortunately, the tattoo artist was booked, so I agreed to come back the following day. After endless hours of searching for tattoo inspirations, I settled on a tattoo concept I thought captured everything I wanted to say to show my love and appreciation for my son. I waited anxiously on a Friday afternoon as the tattoo artist drew up my tattoo then talked through the pain as he inked my work of art onto the left-hand side of my upper back. When he finished, I was so excited to see the completed product.

While this was my third tattoo it was the most memorable of the three. It symbolized me bringing my son along with me wherever I go. I thanked my tattoo artist for his amazing work and asked my husband to snap a picture of the new ink I received. In my excitement, I sent the picture to my mom. She replied, "*wow*," followed by another reply, "*that's big!*" Clearly not the response I was hoping for. I instantly became hurt and upset at her reaction. It was like a slap in the face…which inadvertently seemed like a diss to myself and my son. I couldn't believe her reaction and was very short and standoffish for a couple days.

After cooling off, I decided I needed to let my mom know how I really felt. It was hard, because this was the first time in forever my mom and I had a rift in our relationship. I informed my mom how her initial reaction to my tattoo made me feel. I explained to her that even though the tattoo was a little larger than what she & I expected, it meant a lot to me, and to fit all the intricate details I wanted (his footprints, his name, the date, a heart, and the word love) into the design, it had to be a bit bigger than I had originally planned. I also informed her that her initial reaction seemed dismissive to me, and it hurt my feelings as this was one way I chose to honor my son's memory. While her opinions about the size may have been valid at the time, the way it came across was tough for me to hear in my grieving state. Later, when she saw the tattoo in person, she realized it wasn't as big as she originally thought.

From this scenario, I learned that sometimes our feelings will be hurt unintentionally. We will be angered by something we thought someone should say or shouldn't say, but they say it any way. These moments are teachable moments where you can use your voice to speak up. If there is something you don't like, speak up and say something. If there is something you need... speak up and lay out your needs to help you get through the situation. If you need time to process things, don't be afraid to take a sabbatical and get the much-needed rest and relaxation you need to operate at your highest capacity. When you speak up and take actions on your own, don't feel bad. This is all part of the grief cycle. Also, remember that while dealing with grief, our emotions are often heightened which can allow us to take things out of context and become easily offended. Just remember to keep the lines of communication open, so that you can express how you feel without harboring resentment.

During this time, your needs and wants (based on your mood, emotions etc.) may constantly change. There are some conversations you may need to have to express what you need. Don't shy away from them. Just know they are normal to have. Also, remember it is your responsibility to let people know what it is *you* need from them. Once the request is out there, there is nothing you can do from that point on but wait for a response and then respond accordingly.

Conversations you may need to have, may revolve around these topics:

### Space

You may not want to be around a lot of people when you first lose your baby/child and that is a perfectly normal reaction. Set up an "interceptor" who can intercept calls, visitors, questions and concerns for you so that you're not bothered. When we first lost our son, I created one general Facebook post and sent out text messages to my closest friends. I simply informed them our son gained his angel wings and that we simply wanted prayers from those who were willing to offer them up for us. I also let people know at that time I didn't want any calls or visitors. At that moment, I wasn't in an emotional state to try to "entertain" people with questions and concerns. I was still trying to sort things out and process the entire situation myself. My husband did some of the intercepting for me while I was in the hospital as well as my mom, who came into town and stayed with us for a few days to help us get settled. Find an interceptor you can trust and rely on to inform people of your status and intercept things you may not be ready to talk about or handle.

### Companionship

After losing a child you may feel lonely. Since this isn't something that happens to many people, you automatically feel isolated. That isolation can drive you to seek companionship. Some may shy away from the companion role because they may not have the perfect words to say to you, especially if it never has happened to them, or they may feel uncomfortable around you because they feel they cannot relate to your situation. Let's be honest, deceased babies are taboo. But, let your companion know that they don't have to say anything. A lot of the time, we are just in need of some human interaction. Someone to sit with us while we comb over our thoughts. Someone to be a spring board to sound off feelings of hurt, sadness, grief, and sorrow. A true companion is someone who will just be there when we feel we are at our lowest point.

It is best to seek a companion who will allow you to be yourself always. You may need a shoulder to cry on or you may need a pick me upper. Your companion should never make you feel bad for feeling the way you do. They are there to help assist you through your grief. You may find all you need in one companion or you may have a village of companions that help you through the initial shock of grief. Look for companionship in your spouse, a parent, a close family member or friend; someone who has experienced your type of loss, through a support group, through a church member, or even a counselor. Don't be afraid to be your own companion. Write out your feelings, your mood, your concerns, and your questions in a journal. And use it to track your progress.

### *Intimacy*

Intimacy is something you may crave after losing a child (or multiple children). You try to fill the void of loss through intimacy with someone. That intimacy doesn't necessarily mean you want to get physical (see paragraph on "Sex" for more details on physical intimacy), it may mean you want to be around your spouse more. The intimacy between my husband and I grew through our loss. We communicated more. We shared our raw emotions with each other more often. We allowed each other space. We even leaned on each other more. One thing I was often appreciative of my husband doing, was pulling me into his arms to hold me when he heard me crying at night and letting me lay on his chest. He may not have had the perfect words to say, but that simple gesture of pulling me in and holding me close told me he had my back in this matter. He allowed me to just be me, broken and all. He allowed me space to grieve in my own personalized way. He allowed me to be real with all my emotions, whether it was sadness, confusion, anger, joy, appreciation, etc.

Some may crave intimacy, while others may shun intimacy all together. If you choose the latter of the two options, just know there is nothing wrong with you and your feelings are absolutely valid. If you are pushing away that human connection with someone else, determine why. If you truly don't want to be around someone, that is perfectly fine. But if you are pushing people away when you truly want intimacy, don't be afraid to speak up. Losing your child can feel like you're alone on a deserted island and you don't want to fall down the rabbit hole of feeling like you have no one to turn to. I would suggest finding at least one person whom you can confide in at your lowest moment i.e. your spouse, sibling, mom, dad, or best friend.

### *Sex*

Sex may be a tricky subject after losing your child. Some may want to rush in right away to feel connected to their spouse or partner. You may feel like you want to have sex often to try and get pregnant immediately, so you can fill the void of losing a child. You may shy away from sex all together because the action is a painful reminder of the loss you suffered, not to mention the doctor asks you to refrain from sex for four to six weeks after your delivery. Again, neither choice is right or wrong. But it is best to explain your stance with your partner, so they know exactly what page you are on. You don't want to move too fast or too slow and not have your partner aligned with your plan. Most importantly, you want to discuss why you are taking the stance you are taking. This way, your partner can fully understand why you are or are not engaging in this intimate act. You may even have questions for your doctor, especially if you don't know what caused your baby's death before you resume having sex again. If you need your doctor's advice, be sure to write out all your questions and make an appointment, so you can get the clarity and peace of mind to move forward when you are fully ready.

*Friendship*

During this time, you might experience a shift in some of your friendships. You may be surprised at how people react to the news of you losing your baby. Some people may draw closer to you, creating a deeper bond and friendship, while others may pull away or distance themselves all together. When you're on the front line of the situation, you may feel some type of way at how you are being treated. I will remind you, that while you are dealing with the loss of your child first hand, others, who are connected with you, are trying to cope with your loss as well. While I know their feelings are not your primary concern, their feelings may still be valid.

Be sure to set up boundaries with your friends. Let them know the topics you are comfortable discussing and those that are off limits. Be sure to be upfront about what you can and cannot handle surrounding your loss, even if it may be an uncomfortable conversation for you and them. It may take a little extra effort in the beginning; however, you will be relieved once you set up the parameters to help your friendship blossom during your time of grief. Be honest and up front with your friends when it comes to communication during your time of grief. It can help you avoid some tense moments of miscommunication and misunderstandings.

If your friend is pregnant or becomes pregnant after the loss of your baby, be sure to have an honest conversation. You may be hesitant to be around her as her newborn baby or her baby bump may trigger emotions you don't want to surface. You may even become jealous or envious and not want to spread those emotions or say something that may offend her. Whatever you decide, just be upfront and honest with her. Be sure to speak on the situation from your personal perspective versus using "you" which can instantly place a person on the defensive. Navigating the waters of friendship during your time of loss can be difficult but I promise you, if you are honest about where you are in your journey you will be extended grace. If you are not, you may want to rethink your friendship all together.

### *Support*

If you are in search of support, be sure to know what you are seeking. This will make it easier to align your requests with the support you need. If you want a shoulder to lean on when you cry, think of people who have been there for you in the past or who have stepped up during your loss to reach out to. If you need a listening ear, be sure to find people who will allow you to talk without interruption or false concern. Try support groups, a therapist, a close trusted friend or family member. If you are looking for help, be sure to jot down things you need help with. Some of the things you may need help with that you may not initially consider are:

- **Food** – You may want to tell people if they ask what you need, to send you gift cards, provide food, or send over cooked meals so that it's one less thing you must worry about during your initial wave of grief. When I first left the hospital, my brother ordered take out for us every day for an entire week. I didn't know that was something I needed, but it turned out to be a huge help. I didn't have to think about cooking because he took care of that necessity. What made it even more special, was the fact we didn't even have to ask him to do it. He just did it on his own.

- **Child care for other children you may have** – If you have other children, you may need a grandparent, a nanny, or a family friend to come and take your other children off your hands, giving you an opportunity to grieve alone first. Afterwards, you can incorporate your children into your grief process once you've truly had a chance to work out the loss on your own. They too will be dealing with the loss of their sibling and may have questions. Ask a family member to take the kids out and do something fun/special with them so they are not abandoned during your initial time of grief.

- **Housework/Chores** – You may want to hire someone or solicit a family friend or church member to come over and take care of basic housework: dishes, cooking, laundry, and keeping the house clean. This is another mundane chore that is helpful to have outsourced while you are in your early stages of grieving.

Whatever other support you may need, don't be afraid to speak up and let people know. It is perfectly normal to need help and support physically, mentally, emotionally, and psychologically after suffering from [baby] loss. This is a time when most people will be willing to throw their weight around to help you. The further along you are in your grief journey the more the help will wane, so get it while you can.

*Love*

Feeling some type of love while you're grieving is important. It is important to know you are wanted, you are loved, you are cared for, you are remembered. You should let people know what you need emotionally to feel loved. You may ask for pick-me-uppers like your favorite candy, flowers, or meal. You may ask a friend to accompany you to a movie or play. You may even want to be around little kids or babies to help you cope with your loss. Whatever helps you feel loved and aids in compressing the pain, by all means go for it! One of the most important types of love is SELF-LOVE! It is important that you don't beat yourself up when you may get off track, when you don't feel like moving, when you stay in your pajamas all day, when you bawl your eyes out for a straight hour, or when you feel all alone. Just know that these are normal grief occurrences. Don't beat yourself up. Allow yourself time to grieve and heal. Allow yourself room for mistakes and growth. And most importantly, allow yourself time to experience any emotions you go through.

### *Prayer/Meditation*

Sometimes the only thing you can rely on in your grief is the word of God and prayer. After losing DJ, my prayer life, and time spent in the word, significantly increased. At times, it felt like God was the only person I could lean on. When I found myself in the deepest despair, in the thick of my own grief, I would always look to God and let Him know the honest, unmasked state I was in. I made sure to ask for peace, clarity, and hope, so that I could make it through the day. I can't say these days were not accompanied with a downpour of tears, but I can confess I always felt as if God was there with me even in my suffering. If you do not believe in God, I would find something like meditation to help block out the noise and distractions of grief to help you center your spirit and truly zone out. It can be a truly difficult feat as your mind will be filled with various sentiments about your experience. But push pass the distractions and focus. When you center yourself that is when you can begin to hear God's still voice.

*Finding stress relievers to help you cope with the pain*

It is good practice to find stress relievers to help you cope with the pain of your grief. For some people that could be art, like drawing, painting, and pottery. For others, a stress reliever can be writing. For me, this was very therapeutic, hence me writing this book. The ability to write out my raw, unbiased, unadulterated feelings is like no other. I simply write until I feel like I'm done, then I go back and read some of the writings I've journaled. It is amazing to see how much I've developed and changed over the course of my grief. Some days, I am super optimistic and hopeful and others I am laden with pain and anger. Both of those sides are a piece of me and it is nice to see the transformation right before my eyes. Another stress reliever may be exercise. Some people may enjoy running, lifting weights, and some may even like dance classes (I suggest checking out a local or virtual Zumba class, you will love it)! Don't feel bad for putting your needs first. Find stress relievers that make you feel your best, whether it is in a group setting or you do it solo.

*What is off limits in terms of things people can and cannot bring up to you*

Be sure to also think about the things that are acceptable and off limits for you to talk about. There is no need to get upset when you clearly define the parameters and safe space to make you feel comfortable. For me, talking about the loss of my son was very therapeutic. By recounting the experience and sharing my journey, not only with my close family and friends, but with my followers on social media as well, I was able to better cope with my loss. Constantly talking about DJ also made him feel more real and helped me to solidify his memory. I realized for me, talking about my son put me in a space of happiness. While the story didn't end how I wanted it to, the thought of my son's face, his long fingers, big feet, and simply remembering our birth journey brings me joy. I will tell the story to anyone willing to listen. I don't mind my family or friends asking questions because it makes me feel more connected with DJ.

While I am an open book, my husband is the total opposite. He didn't want to show anyone my son's pictures. He didn't like to talk about him much to people outside of me, and he didn't like sharing our experience on any social media platforms. Our approaches of coping are on two total opposite ends of the spectrum, yet neither is wrong. They are simply what individually works for us in our grieving journeys. Be sure to figure out what boundaries you will allow, and which ones are deal breakers. Let people know up front what you are willing to talk about pertaining to your child/children and be sure to spell it out, so they know what is on the table and what is completely off limits. Be ready to answer the tough questions. When people, typically strangers who don't know our back-story, ask us if we have children, we agreed we would say no. When family members talk about DJ, I want them to reference him as our angel baby and call him by name. Although he is not physically here on earth, he was and still is a huge part of our lives. I want people to remember him as such. He wasn't just a ghost passing through the night. He was a real human I held in my arms.

Be sure to take the lead when it comes to dealing with how to reference your child. You are the guardian of their legacy. You have the right to make the rules. If you want people to talk about your child openly and often then do so. If you'd rather not bring up your child and keep them as a quiet keepsake in your personal memory bank, that is fine as well. Whatever you decide, just know you are the captain of your own ship. Don't feel bad either way.

### *Triggers*

Beware there may be words, sights, smells, or noises that may trigger or incite some type of reaction out of you. You may not even recognize them at first, but once you begin to familiarize yourself with grief, you will notice that these triggers can be triggered at any moment and they can come and go just like the soft subtle breeze passing by you on a sandy beach. Keep track of what triggers expose positive reactions and those that incite negative attitudes and moods. Triggers are different for everyone. For me, when I saw a newborn baby, I was more in awe of that precious gift, but when I saw a woman with a baby bump it triggered the emotion of sadness and even anger because my time with my bump was cut short. It is good to identify these types of triggers, so that you know what to do when they occur. It also allows you to come up with a backup plan when these triggers occur. Common triggers to look out for are:

- Commercials with babies in them
- Songs that remind you of your child/children you lost
- The baby aisle at stores you frequent
- Public bathroom stalls that have changing stations
- The doctor's office or hospital where you received the news your baby did not make it

- The doctor or ultrasound technician that administered your ultrasound to confirm your baby no longer had a heartbeat
- TV shows that incorporate storylines where actors/actresses lose their child/children
- Friends or family who are pregnant the same time as you or who become pregnant after you who go on to have healthy living babies
- Women with baby bumps
- Seeing babies that are around the age your baby "should have been"
- Seeing babies that were younger than your baby who were born prematurely (with or without complications) that survived
- Seeing baby strollers, car seats, playpens, etc., or any other baby products
- Hearing crying or laughing babies
- Seeing others pregnancy announcements on social media (especially right when you log in or scroll down your timeline)
- Getting emails and updates on how far along you should be from pregnancy apps, blogs, and websites you signed up for while you were pregnant
- Pictures of your sleeping angel
- Ultrasound pictures, baby bump pictures, or anything that reminds you of your sleeping angel
- People who complain about their children when you just lost yours
- People who ask, "when are you going to have a baby?"

- People who assume you're still pregnant because you haven't lost your baby weight yet
- Seeing stretch marks on your body with no baby to account for the physical damage done
- People who suggest you can always try again (like your baby is replaceable)
- Having a close friend experience pregnancy while you mourn the loss of your child
- Working in an environment where a lot of children or babies are present
- Having your milk come in, and dealing with engorged breasts even though you have no baby to nurse

### *Concerning reactions to triggers*

Besides the triggers listed above, there are also concerning triggers that you should be cognizant of when you are trying to tread the murky waters of grief. It is crucial that you red flag responses or behaviors to these specific triggers that can cause you to spiral in the wrong direction or even worse that can be fatal if they go unchecked. Although I did not experience any of these extreme behaviors sparked by a trigger, I feel it is my duty to keep these toxic behaviors on your radar, so you can avoid potential pitfalls. Some of those concerning reactions to triggers include, but are not limited to:

- Experimenting with drugs

- Drinking excessive amounts of alcohol

- Being surrounded by toxic people, who do not have your best interest at heart or influence you to do/or say the wrong things

- People who make you feel bad, sad, angry etc. with their words

- People who just want to be around you to be nosey (non – trustworthy people)

- Places or things that make you sad or put you in a negative head space

- Babies or children (if they trigger negative emotions inside you)

- Songs, places, smells, sounds etc.

- Suicidal thoughts

- Harmful actions to yourself

- Violence to yourself or others

- Dangerous living (i.e. having sex with random people unprotected, drinking and driving, reckless driving or behavior, fighting etc.)

If you identify with any of these behaviors and begin to become triggered and impacted in a negative way, please seek professional help from a trusted source, so you can deal with your loss in a healthy and safe environment without doing harm to yourself or others.

### How you will recognize your child in the context of your family

It's good to know how you want your child recognized in the context of your family. Some may not recognize a child they loss through stillbirth, while others will have a name, a gravesite (or an urn filled with their babies ashes from cremation), a memorial of some sort at their home and much more. No one can tell you how you should recognize your own child. For some, it may be best to only recognize children that are living on this earth, while some of us would prefer counting and referencing the number of earthly and heavenly children we possess. Neither choice is incorrect. It is a matter of preference and what makes you comfortable and happy at the end of the day. You also may want to think about how people refer to you regarding your child. If this was your only child that died, do you still want to be viewed as a mother or father? Do you think of yourself as a parent? Do you want people to recognize you on holidays such as Mother's and Father's Day? These are questions that you should search inside yourself for answers, so when these scenarios arise, you will be prepared to handle them. There is nothing worse than being caught off guard, especially while you're grieving, because grief already has a mind of its own. It's best to try to control what you can as best as possible.

### How you will talk about your child in a real-world setting

To keep from being caught off guard, knowing how you will respond to certain questions about your baby is helpful to think about in advance. It is best to think about answers to the following questions, so you won't be embarrassed, upset or blindsided:

1.  Do you have any children? If so how many?

2.  When are you going to start having children?

3.  Are you going to try again for another baby?

4.  Do you want a boy or a girl?

5.  What happened to your baby?

6.  *If people don't know you lost your baby, they may ask...* Where is your baby? How old is your baby now? What's your baby's name?

There are a host of other questions people can ask. Typically, I get asked questions 1, 2, 3 and 6 most often. Depending on who is asking the question, complete stranger versus acquaintance or friend, will slightly skew the response. Just have an answer prepared, just in case. It is also good to take into consideration the age of the person asking the question. Kids may want to know why did your baby have to die? Or why did your baby go live in heaven? You must be prepared for questions such as these. The more prepared you are, the easier it is to answer the questions and the less likely you are to be caught off guard or worse offended. As I've heard, you won't have to get ready, if you stay ready. Be ready to be approached with questions that may make you feel a bit uneasy.

*How will you carry on the legacy of your baby?*

You should also think about how you want to remember your baby. While I will have a full chapter on this subject later in the book (Chapter 13: Carrying on Your Angel's Legacy, page 174), I think it is best to really think about how you want to remember your baby. Do you want something small to remember your munchkin's life, or do you want something grandiose? Like most sections in this book state it truly depends on you, your spouse, your family, and how you see fit to honor the legacy of your child.

# *Chapter* 7

## Grief's Rollercoaster

*"Now may the Lord of peace Himself*
*continually grant you peace in every circumstance.*
*The Lord be with you all!"*
*– 2 Thessalonians 3:16 New American Standard Bible*

In the eye of the storm of my grief, I was aimlessly searching to find answers how to better cope. I also wanted to find information to help understand my grief on a deeper level. Through my searching I discovered the Kubler – Ross Model of The Five Stages of Grief (PhD, 2018). This model breaks grief down into five basic stages:

1. **Shock and Denial**
   a. Avoidance
   b. Confusion
   c. Fear
   d. Numbness
   e. Blame
2. **Anger**
   a. Frustration
   b. Anxiety
   c. Irritation
   d. Embarrassment
   e. Shame
3. **Depression and Detachment**
   a. Overwhelmed
   b. Blahs
   c. Lack of energy
   d. Helplessness
4. **Dialogue and Bargaining**
   a. Reaching out to others
   b. Desire to tell one's story
   c. Struggle to find meaning for what has happened
5. **Acceptance**
   a. Exploring options
   b. A new plan in place
   c. Empowerment
   d. Security
   e. Self – Esteem
   f. Meaning

Through these five stages, comes a very diverse wave of emotions and reactions. As I've discussed throughout this book, the process of first learning my son had no heartbeat to now has been a journey. I've experienced many emotions on grief's rollercoaster. At one point or another, on this journey, I've experienced pit stops at all these destinations on grief's rollercoaster. One thing I've learned, is the fact that the cycles of grief doesn't necessarily mean grief will occur in a cyclical pattern. I also learned that an individual's grief journey may appear "out of order." You may skip some steps in grief that another person experiences. Knowing what grief has to offer makes it a tad bit easier to identify when it occurs. Additionally, it can be a helpful tool to overcome its various phases.

Go through the grief stages and identify where you are, where you want to go, and those areas where you feel you struggle. By knowing what is ahead of you and seeing where you've come from, you've enabled yourself to sort out exactly what you are feeling as you travel through the five stages. As mentioned previously in this chapter, I experienced each stage of grief at some point during my journey. Each one came about on its own timing, and more times than not, happened out of the blue. Here are some recounts of behaviors that occurred under each classified emotional group.

### Shock and Denial

Upon learning about the passing of DJ, I was in total shock and confused. I could not understand how I woke up the morning of January 15, 2016 twenty-eight weeks pregnancy with the excitement of being a new mommy, twelve weeks away from the finish line, only to return to bed that evening as a grieving mother who had the task of delivering the deceased child she hoped, dreamed, and prayed for the following day. I was numb to the experience at first. I felt like a ton of bricks were dumped on me and knocked me out for the count.

While I did not experience **avoidance** or **fear** during my stage of shock and denial, I immediately started playing the **blame game**, blaming myself for causing my son's life to be cut short. It seemed like the obvious choice to blame myself, since I was the vehicle in which my son's life depended upon. I was the person who was supposed to provide the safe, warm, protected space for DJ to grow. I was supposed to be the one who provided the nutrients needed for DJ to gain strength. But instead of being a safe place of refuge for my growing baby, it became a war zone for my child, ultimately creating a casualty of war with the sacrifice of my little angel.

This was a tough stage of grief for me. I had to confront my worst nightmare head on, losing my child while being pregnant. I had to say out loud that my son was no longer living. I had to come to grasps that my first-born son would only become a distant memory in my mind as I was asked to do the insurmountable of delivering his lifeless body into the world and saying hi and goodbye all within twenty-four hours.

After the shock and denial stage started to fade, after I delivered my angel, held him in my arms, prayed for him, rededicated him back to God, and kissed him goodbye, my grief morphed into anger.

### *Anger*

I am, in no way, shape, or form, proud of my moments of anger, however, this is a natural part of grieving. The anger stage comes with a gamut of emotions, and I experienced each of them one by one. The first emotion to latch onto my psyche was **frustration**. I was frustrated by the fact that I was cremating my son when I should have been planning my son's baby shower and preparing his nursery. Instead of getting ready for one of life's happiest moments, I was now trying to pick up the million and one shattered pieces of my life, and slowly put them back together to try and create a resemblance of my past life prior to DJ's death. Through the frustration of my loss, I began to experience **irritation**, which in turn caused me to lash out at others...mainly my husband. I would be having a decent day, and then the smallest triggers would occur and instantly put me in a sour, sucky mood. When those mood swings occurred, I would become angry and project those negative emotions onto my husband. I truly apologize now, for the way I acted towards him at the crux of my anger. He didn't deserve such treatment as he was also trying to grapple with the fact that we had lost our son...his namesake. Usually in my angry haste, I would snap or use a sarcastic remark. I would even shut down completely with an attitude.

Since I'm usually a happy, positive person, this phase of grief really took a toll on me. Constantly dealing with the irritation, anger, and the frustration was tough, but it was my reality for some time. After moving from the steps of anger, I began to experience **embarrassment** and **shame**. I was embarrassed at the fact that I had announced to the world, via various social media platforms, that I was expecting a bundle of joy only to have to abort my initial excitement with my tail between my legs. That embarrassment of loss, after publicly expressing my elation of expecting, led to shame. The one thing my body was supposed to do naturally...bear a healthy child...failed me!

If you are having a rough time navigating the anger stage of grief as I did, give yourself grace. You are human. You are allowed to feel each emotion that comes with the desolation of losing a child!

### *Depression and Detachment*

During my time spent in the depression and detachment phase of grief, I experienced being **overwhelmed**, a case of the "**blahs**," a **lack of energy**, and **helplessness**. I don't think I had a full-blown case of diagnosed depression per se, but I remember feeling each of these emotions at some point during my grief journey.

I was slightly overwhelmed with my loss. It occurred smack dab in the middle of my last semester of my senior year in college. My loss occurred while I was dream-chasing, trying to obtain my second bachelor's degree in Apparel Textile Technology, coupled with a minor in Business Administration, and trying to maintain a 4.0 grade point average that I worked so hard to sustain. Talk about a tough task. Then on top of juggling my raw emotions of loss and my senior year work load, I had other responsibilities at school as I held leadership positions in two separate organizations. I was heavily involved in a few ministries at my church: the tutoring ministry, children and youth volunteer, great girls' ministry leader for middle and high school aged girls, as well as a praise team leader/member. Furthermore, I still had to maintain emotional intimacy with my husband and take care of my wifely duties at home (cooking, cleaning, laundry, etc.). To say I was overwhelmed was an understatement.

To combat being overwhelmed, I forced myself to prioritize the most important things in my life at that moment. Once things were prioritized, I stepped away from some of my responsibilities, so I could focus on self-care and try to regain some type of balance. Give yourself permission to walk away from things that may be overbearing while you are trying to grieve. You will feel better when you slow down, cut out the distractions, and focus inward to begin your healing process.

My case of the "blahs" and lack of energy were coupled together. Before I forced myself to step away from some of my responsibilities, I began to feel uninspired, unfocused, and downright drained from the emotional beating I was taking nightly from my baby loss experience. Those feelings of being uninspired turned into an attitude of not caring. This is where the case of the blahs entered. Nothing seemed as important as it once did. Life lost its luster and zeal. I was tired and drained of energy because every night I would cry for hours before finally forcing myself to go to sleep. This happened nonstop for a couple months straight.

I remember a specific time when my feelings of being overwhelmed, a case of the blahs, and my lack of energy all collided into a huge case of helplessness. It was a few weeks after I had given birth to my sleeping angel. I received an invitation to my cousin's birthday celebration. She had a swanky get together at an upscale restaurant/lounge in Atlanta. I remember contemplating for hours, before the party began, if I should go. I wrestled with the fact that I needed to get out the house, so I could get my mind off my loss, but on the flip side, I didn't know if I was emotionally ready to be surrounded with small talk and mingling. Against my better judgement, I decided to go to the birthday celebration. While the party turned out great, and I did have a pretty good time getting out and socializing for a couple hours, as soon as I got back into the car my grief swallowed me whole.

As I drove back to my brother's house, surrounded by a black midnight sky, I remember hearing "I Will Always Love You" by Whitney Houston on the radio, which is one of my trigger songs. I immediately burst into tears. While the song was on, I remember seeing the bright lights of a semi-truck coming toward me in the distance. In that split second of helplessness, I grappled with the thought of just swerving in front of that semi to end my life, to take away the deep-rooted pain I felt with the loss of my angel. As the semi and I passed in the night, and I saw his taillights in my rearview mirror, I remember being surprised at the dark turn of my thoughts. It was the first time in my life that the thought of suicide crossed my mental frequency. When I reached my brother's house, I sat in the driveway and bawled my eyes out. The loss of my baby truly changed me and for a moment altered my mind, attitude, and outlook on life. But the good news is…I did not stay in that place of helplessness for too long. I restored my mind over time and could look at my loss through new lenses. It was a process, but I am a living witness that God can turn around any situation, including baby loss.

So, if you are feeling absolutely defeated and even considering taking your own life to silence the pain…**HANG ON, IN THERE!** The pain may seem unbearable, but if you give yourself time, I promise you, you will make it to the other side of loss.

### Dialogue and Bargaining

The dialogue and bargaining phase is when I truly began to see the light at the end of the tunnel. After experiencing my suicidal thought, I confided in my husband, telling him my deep dark secret that ending my life crossed my mind in that moment of passing the semi. I didn't feel like I was coping like I should with the loss of my munchkin, so I asked him to help me find a grief therapist that could help me steer the ship through the choppy waters of grief. To have my husband's support and blessing in finding a therapist was the push I needed to seek help.

When I finally reached out for help and started talking about my situation with my therapist and others, I began to look at my situation from a different vantage point. My therapist offered a third-party view which allowed her to offer me advice from a whole new perspective. Her quiet voice of reason pushed me to explore my deep feelings, to create a plan for healing, and to do the work to get to the other side of grief. With her guided assistance and my transparency about my loss, it began to help those burdens become lighter. Although I still shed tears, it wasn't as often, and I was able to objectively look at my tears and emotions as just something that was a part of my journey, instead of thinking of my emotions as weaknesses. With my therapist's help, I began to unpack why I believe my family was chosen for this insuperable mission. She helped me use the revelation as fuel to step into my purpose of spreading joy, hope, and love to families who have experienced the same tragic fate as me and my husband. Hence, the writing of this book/memoir about my loss through stillbirth.

*Acceptance*

After experiencing the first four phases of grief, I'm finally able to say I'm in my acceptance phase of grief. I no longer cry every day. I no longer look at my situation through the prism of sadness. I no longer mope around because I've discovered my purpose through this grief journey. I realized God allowed me to go through this experience of loss, so I could share my story and help others heal by facilitating a space to openly discuss the highs and lows of baby loss in a safe way. He's given me a new-found purpose. He's allowed me to enjoy the little things in life that I may not have noticed prior to DJ's death. He's given me a new plan (this book is only the beginning, so stay tuned) and a new sense of empowerment. I no longer live in a constant state of fear of failure, after going through hell and back, I know I can confidently conquer the world or any situation as long as God is by my side. God has also given me a sense of security in my faith, in my relationship with Him, and in my strengthened marriage. I've also gained a new level of self-esteem that lets me know I was brought to this earth with a predestined purpose. God knew, before I was even born, I would lose DJ, yet and still He ordained the purpose that this tragic situation would have on my life, which in turn gave my life an entire new meaning.

As you can see, grief truly is a roller coaster with a ton of dips, drops, twists, and turns. At times, you may be on top of the hill with vision beyond belief, but other times you may be stuck in the valley, where all you can do is look up to God for strength. No matter where you are in the journey hold on and enjoy the ride.

You may not have experienced some of the side effects of grief I experienced emotionally, but it doesn't mean that your grief journey is more or less valid than mine or any other grieving parent. As I've stressed countless times in this book, no two grieving stories look alike, no matter who you've lost (child, parent, spouse, friend etc.). This chapter serves as a reminder that the stages of grief are commonplace. Many grieving parents will experience these raw emotions that you may or may not have been ready for. But just buckle up and raise your hands up high as the ride begins to take off. Once you're docked in the station, and you've completed grief's roller coaster, you will look back and marvel at how far you've come!

# Chapter 8

## Dealing With Grief (Her Story)

*"17 The righteous cry, and the Lord hears
And delivers them out of all their troubles.
18 The Lord is near to the brokenhearted and
saves those who are crushed in spirit."*
– **Psalm 34:17-18** *New American Standard
Bible*

The only time my husband's and my outer displays of grief aligned, was the day we found out DJ no longer had a heartbeat, and the day we had to say our final goodbyes. Outside of these two isolated events, our grief stories have looked completely different ever since. One thing you must keep in your mind about grief and dealing with loss, is that it is a personal journey. No two grief stories look exactly alike. They might have some underlying similarities, but no one experiences grief the same way even if they are grieving for the same person. There are even noted differences between how men and women grieve. Neither reaction to loss holds more weight, it just is how each individual gender handles their own sorrow and grief operating within the confines of societal norms.

The first day we found out we had lost our sweet angel, my initial reaction was to break down, while my husband's coping mechanism was to hold everything together. As the analytical thinker in the family, he wanted the answers to "*what do we do next?*" He needed a step-by-step guide on how to rectify the situation. Me on the other hand… I reacted from an emotional place. The details weren't as important as dealing with the fact that my poor baby died in my care. The only thing I could mutter to my husband, amongst the tears, was a continuous flow of "I'm Sorrys!" I felt horrible for my son who didn't have enough fluid around him to survive, for my husband who would never get to see his namesake grow up and conquer the world, and for myself for losing a part of me.

My grief story started on Friday, January 15, 2016 and has since been a part of my everyday life. There has not been one day that has passed that I haven't thought about my son in one capacity or another. Grief has become a lifelong passenger on my journey of life. At times this passenger is quietly sitting in the backseat while other times it is loudly demanding to drive. While I wish, I could say that grief has not truly affected me, I must be candid and say it has truly transformed my entire life. Grief sometimes swallows me whole and drowns me in its sorrow. Other times, it reminds me of the good times and offers glimpses of places where I should insert gratefulness. Grief is sometimes hard to put into words because you simply can't describe the pain or mood you are in, nor do you have the right words to make others understand. To conquer grief is to accept the fact that it will never go away, but it will morph into different states of being along the way. As I stated previously, my grief started with an outer emotional display of sadness, confusion, and pure heartbreak. My grief then turned into anger. From there it moved into discovery, and then into gratitude and thankfulness.

One thing that can be mentioned about grief, is that it is circular. It is a never-ending wheel of emotions that is constantly turning, moving, and rotating. At times, you like where the grief wheel lands (i.e. peace, humbleness, gratitude, thankfulness, reflection etc.). Other times, you feel like you are one lose screw from becoming completely unhinged. Grief is an intricate balance of being sane and being coocoo for cocoa puffs. Before entering the doctor's office on January 15, I had never truly experienced loss so up-close and personal. I had lost an uncle, great aunts and uncles, cousins, class/schoolmates and my paternal grandparents (one which died prior to my birth and the other passed when I was just one year old). Overall, I had skated through the game of life unscathed by the grief monster. But on the fifteenth of the first month of a new year, my artificial house of brick turned into one of glass. My world came crashing down. Let's face it, grief is horrible no matter how you slice it, but the part that hurt me the most, was the fact that I was so blissfully unprepared for its arrival.

As a baby loss mom grief for me has manifested itself in a host of ways, mainly through tears, journaling, blogging, anger, questioning, conversation, envy, counseling, prayer, and connection. Although these outward displays of grief may not mimic yours, it is a good idea to identify the outward displays of grief you experience so you know how to combat them when they arise.

*Tears*

A huge part of my grief journey has been to openly welcome the sadness that comes along with the loss of a child. I had to acknowledge that this sadness, while mostly hidden from others, could appear at any moment or be triggered by the slightest thing in the strangest places. The biggest thing I've learned and continue to learn is that you shouldn't fight your feelings of sadness or moments of weakness. They are neither bad nor good they just are. When I feel the sadness well up from within and the stream of tears begin to fall, I just ride the emotional wave like a surf board. I cry because I miss my son tremendously; I cry because of the things I will never get to experience with my son; I cry because I sometimes feel helpless; and I cry because it helps me release the pent-up emotions I hold inside. Sometimes, the tears may singularly fall for a moment or they may cascade down my face for hours upon end. However long it takes, I just allow it to happen because I know it is all a part of the process. I don't beat myself up for it. I acknowledge it, ride the emotional roller coaster, pick myself up and try to move forward as best I can. Just remember while this is an endless process, it does get better with time.

*Journaling*

Journaling has been a very significant part of my grief process. Ever since I found out about the loss of my son, I began journaling on a regular basis. It truly helped to journal and dump out all my raw emotions and feelings. Sometimes the feelings you have may not be the most PC. However, when you write them down, you acknowledge that they are what you are feeling in the moment, you allow yourself to be real with you, and you release those feelings of anger, confusion, sadness, despair, depression, and can begin to replace them with hope, love, gratitude, and thankfulness. One thing that journaling helped me see is how God can take a bleak situation and turn it around. The pain from the loss of my son will always be there, but I have begun to look at it from a lens of gratitude more so than sadness. Through this pain, I've gained a bevy of benefits. Journaling made me begin to realize that I can use this experience to either tear me down or go to higher heights which I never would have imagined possible prior to DJ's passing. Chronicling my grief journey also enabled me to see that the further I became removed from the loss, the more "stable" life became. That doesn't mean I don't have days where I am down in the dumps, they just become less frequent. One of the biggest benefits of journaling is being able to look back and see how far you've come. You can monitor your grief progress from a bird's eye view which helps you to cultivate your testimony and operate from a place of thankfulness for all you've endured and made it through!

### Blogging/Social Media

Using my blog and social media platforms to express my true feelings have been a godsend. In the beginning, I used these platforms as another method of healing, but in the end I gained so much more. Through my honest expression of hurt, pain, and sadness, I was able to connect with people on a deeper level. I used platforms that are typically used to showcase our lives in the best light to share my most difficult and darkest days. I didn't do it for sympathy or to say woe is me; I simply used it to chronicle my true feelings of loss and hurt. Through my honesty, I became a beacon of light to people who were struggling with various hardships and heartaches in their lives, some of whom I didn't even know. It truly touched me to know that even in my lowest state, God used my loss as a light to help others. It has been an incredible journey to see God use my baby loss as a testimony. And it simply happened because I was honest with God, myself, and others. I am not saying just go out and share your story on social media to the masses (because everyone does not have your best interest at heart), but I am saying expressing your true feelings freely about your loss can truly help you grow. It allows you to face your loss head on and deal with all the baggage that comes along with sharing your intimate story of loss. And while you are growing in the process, you may silently be helping someone else heal through your positive and honest actions.

I'd like to share with you just a snippet of some of the social media comments I received in response to being transparent in my grief journey.

*"Alishia, I just want to reach out and say that you and your family have been in my thoughts and prayers! I hope this message finds you well! I cannot imagine what you have been through. Your strength and faith are so admirable! Many blessings to you."* – **Facebook message from a high school classmate**

*"I just read your blog. You never cease to amaze me with your writing. I know that weekend [that you lost DJ] was the worse of your life, but I am so proud of the young woman that you have become. I look forward to your testimony from this whole ordeal! Stand still and know that He is GOD! Love ya!."* – **Text message received from a cousin**

*"You, inside and out, and your positivity is absolutely beautiful. You put a smile on my face. Love ya much Pooh!"* – **Text message received after my parents read a blog post about DJ**

*"And this is why I admire you! The inspiration that came to me by reading your testimony of triumph through your trial is amazing. Thank you!"* – **Comment on Instagram after a follower/friend read a blog post**

*"I admire you more and more each day. Not only do I love your look, I love your message. I wish your resilience could be bottled up and sold. Great [blog] post."* – **Comment on blog from a close collegiate friend**

*"Your strength and courage to be able to share your experience which I know God will turn into your testimony is amazing! You will definitely be in my prayers. Thank you for still finding a way to inspire others in the midst of your storm. Super cute outfit [by the way]!"* – **Comment on blog from a loyal Ali's Fashion Sense reader/follower**

*"Been thinking about and earnestly praying for you and your husband. I'm glad to see you finding a bit of sunshine too...beautiful as always."* – **Comment on blog from a collegiate friend**

As you can see, candidly sharing my story of loss opened the floodgates of feedback that I couldn't have imagined. Believe it or not, on the days I was having the toughest of times, these comments, and countless more, helped me make it through...if only for a moment. You never know who your story will resonate with once you share it. I'm not saying you have to share your story with everyone you encounter, but just know that you may be surprised how many people look at you in your weakest hour and gather that you are powerful and full of strength because of your willingness to share exactly what you are going through.

### *Anger*

While I don't get angry too often, I do notice that there are moments when my mood will change in the blink of an eye. It is something that is still unexplainable to me. But something subconsciously triggers the anger emotion and it puts me in a bad mood. I was never fully angry at God to the point of turning my back on Him or my faith, but I did not understand why He would allow something so tragic to happen to me. I still don't understand the why, but I see how God has used my situation to grow me, my relationship with my husband, my family, friends and much more. I try not to let anger boggle me down, but I don't run away from it either. Just as I do when the tears come, if anger arises, I acknowledge its place, go through the motions, and let it go. I never try to suppress an emotion because it's neither good or bad, if I don't try to harm myself or someone else in the process. If I'm dealing with anger, I usually write it down in my journal, so I can release it and let it go.

I must admit my husband dealt with a lot of my mood changes from perfectly normal to irritation to anger, and he always took it in stride. He totally understood that the anger usually arose from something triggered and that it was not directed toward him but more of the way that my grief sometimes manifested itself in my life. I am so grateful to him, more than words can express. He continues to allow me to grieve in my own way without any judgement or hesitation. It makes it a lot easier to be my authentic self during this process. If you find yourself becoming angry as a symptom of your grief, try to find a quiet place where you can be alone and sort out your anger. Write it down, yell it out, or find some form of exercise or physical activity to participate in. Whatever you need to do to get rid of it, do it; as long as you don't harm yourself or others in the process.

## *Questioning*

As you see in Chapter 4: The Never Ending Why (page 54), questioning was a part of my grief story. It allowed me to release all my frustrations in the form of questions to try to get to the root of my emotions toward loss. This line of questioning also gave me permission to see what areas I needed to work on in my grieving process. It also allows me to see where the hurt still lies, where I have improved or regressed emotionally, and it gives me topics to bring up during my prayer time. When I ask 'why' questions, it is my way of dealing with the hurt. At the end of the day, most of the questions stem from my hurt feelings. I use this method of questioning to express my hurt in an honest and raw way. As a suggestion from my therapist, I jotted down all my questions and tried to come up with possible answers for them as a closure technique. Some of the questions can never be answered, but it's a way to make sense of the life-altering events in a constructive way. I know this exercise can never bring back the child you lost, but it can help you begin your healing process.

## *Conversation*

Conversation has been an amazing part of healing during my grief journey. I like to tell my son's stillbirth story because it allows me to talk about the most amazing human I helped to create, and it allows me to get the story out instead of pinning it up and holding it inside. The idea of releasing the story into the world is such a freeing experience. It validates my son was truly here on this earth, but it also gives my son's life importance when I talk about him, and makes me appreciate the experience, because at the end of the day, I was able to bond with my son, even if only for a few hours before we said our final goodbyes. Holding a conversation about DJ makes me feel closer to him as his mother, and as the vessel that carried him from earth to heaven. It's an unexplainable feeling. I talk about my son every chance I get because it keeps him in the forefront of my memory and draws me closer to him in spirit. Talking about a deceased baby may make some people uncomfortable. But you have to make decisions based on your happiness and sanity when you're in the throes of your grief journey. Some people may not want to talk about your baby because it is a sensitive, uncomfortable, taboo topic in their eyes, but you should simply explain to them that although your baby lost his/her life, they still were a person and very important to you. I simply told my family and friends that talking about DJ truly helped me cope with his loss in so many ways. I am grateful that they allowed me and continue to allow me to talk about and reminisce about him openly. This helps with closure and provides healing in my grief journey.

### Jealousy/Envy

Envy creeps its way into my grief journey. I don't like when it comes but it is a true feeling that occurs from time to time. It is natural to long for your baby after a loss. Seeing other mothers with newborns while you come home empty-handed can be a tough pill to swallow. Know that the sight of pregnant moms or moms with their babies/children may spark something within you. Jealousy and envy can rear their ugly heads and cause you to spiral if you don't get a grasp on it early. I try not to give permission for jealousy and envy to stay camped out in my life for too long. I do however acknowledge that seeing women with their newborns, or shopping in the baby aisle, or mommies posting their cute baby bump or baby's pictures on social media sometimes strike a nerve within me. When these feelings of jealousy arise, I try to replace them with gratefulness. When I see women hold their newborns, I go back to the day I got to hold my newborn, even if he was "sleeping" peacefully. Although he was a sleeping angel, the fact I got to hold him and spend time with him, truly meant a lot. If you experience jealously and envy during your grief journey do not feel bad. It is part of your personal journey. Use it as fuel to dig deep and identify why you may be jealous or envious of the person. Then try to find ways you can spin that jealously into thankfulness inside your hurt. This may be one of the toughest exercises to do, but I promise, once you learn how to combat your jealousy and envy in a positive and constructive way, it will make a world of a difference.

### *Counseling*

Some people can sort out their grief on their own, but others may find it more appealing to go through grief with a guide. When my grief journey seemed to get worse and worse after the loss of my son, I asked my husband if he thought it would be a good idea for me to get a grief counselor. I'd never been to therapy before, but I felt this was a personal step I needed to take to help me improve my footing and gain closure. I began to search for a counselor that would be a good fit and was blessed to find a free counselor through my counseling department at school that was funded through my paid tuition as a KSU student. My counselor was awesome! I liked to talk to her about the situation because she offered a third-party view that was unbiased and structured. She always gave me honest feedback that helped me look at my situation from an alternative perspective. The exercises she provided always had an end goal in mind to help me move forward. She helped me understand that grief is something that subsides with time. She warned me that grief never fully goes away, but she assured me that it would get better. She also helped me work through feelings of being lost, feelings of guilt, shame, hurt, and much more. She encouraged me to find ways to express myself through my grief and was a big cheerleader, support, and guide to help me finish up my school year strong and on track. I am forever indebted to Dr. Holly Brown and how she was a sounding board for me to voice my frustrations, concerns, hurts, and small victories. I truly appreciate her more than words can express.

The first time around, some counseling experiences are not smooth. One therapist does not fit all. Do your research. I suggest looking for a therapist that fits your own needs. Be diligent about what it is you want to gain from each session. With me, I needed someone who wasn't so close to the situation, to be a listening ear and to offer suggestions and commentary on things I was struggling with at the time. It's good to have an end game in mind when you start counseling. I utilized my counselor's expertise in navigating grief to cope with a fresh loss while simultaneously starting my last semester of college. It was the balance I needed to help me emotionally release while staying on track with my studies.

If you get a counselor who is not the right fit for you and your situation, do not hesitate to speak up or find a new one. Your counselor or therapist should be a tool to help you during your grief, not a hindrance that stunts your growth. Don't be afraid to voice what you need from your counselor and come up with a grief plan that can help you heal the best way you see fit. Most of all, be patient with yourself and your therapist. The relationship won't happen overnight. You may need a little time to get comfortable with the counselor but if things do not improve, don't be afraid to search for exactly who and what you need. This is truly about you and helping you move forward. Remember you are your biggest advocate when on the hunt for a therapist.

### *Prayer*

Finally, prayer has been a huge part of my healing during my grief journey. It seemed whenever I was at my lowest points of grief, I would use prayer as a tool to voice my cares, my frustrations, my sadness, my pain, my despair, my grief, my anger, and my jealousy to God. I would lay all my emotions at His feet and ask Him to replace them with love, understanding, gratefulness, a new perspective, optimism, hope, and joy. There are still days I just feel down in the dumps, but the Lord has granted me peace and understanding through this grief journey.

Even on your most difficult days, be kind to yourself. Allow yourself to feel the raw feelings you're feeling. Ask God, or whatever higher power you believe in, to move you from grief to joy; from sadness to gratefulness. Ask Him to direct your path and lead you down the journey of grief with grace. Although it may take some time, remember things will get better.

### *10 Things to Remember About Your Grief Journey*

1. There are various stages of grief.

2. Grief is constantly evolving. It is ever-changing and fluid.

3. Grief sometimes has no rhyme or reason so just go with the flow.

4. One moment you will be on life's mountain peak and the next moment you can be in the deepest valley of despair. Just remember nothing lasts forever.

5. No two grief stories are the same. Don't compare your progress and setbacks to someone else's. We all display our hurt and pain differently and that is perfectly fine!

6. Don't try to suppress or hold back the emotions that accompany your grief. Use your emotions constructively to help you move forward. In the words of Disney's Elsa from *Frozen* "Let it go," but only when you are ready.

7. Don't go on your grief journey alone. Bring someone or a group of people with you for support (i.e. spouse, partner, therapist, parent, friend, pastor, sibling, aunt or uncle, etc.).

8. If you need additional professional help, don't be afraid to ask for it. There is nothing wrong with seeking outside aid to help you feel better.

9. Ask people for support. Spell out the things you need from them and what it looks like, so they can

be clear how they can most effectively support you.

10. Be kind to yourself. This grief journey can be very tough to endure. If you fall back into a state of grief you don't want to be in, don't beat yourself up. Do what you need to do to help you stop, turn around and move in a positive direction.

"Child loss is not an event; it is an indescribable journey of survival!"

— Unknown Author

# Chapter 9

## Dealing With Grief (His Story)

*"God is our refuge and strength,*
*an ever–present help in trouble."*
– **Psalm 46:1** *New American Standard Bible*

As I mentioned in previous chapters, no two grief stories are equivalent, especially when you factor in gender. It is a known fact that men and women grieve quite differently after the loss of a child. As the woman, you may be the one who bottles up all your emotions, while your husband/partner may want to talk through the glaring issues engulfed by loss.

You may find that your spouse wants to take down all remnants of your baby immediately to help him grapple with your sleeping angel's death quicker, while you on the other hand, may cling on to those physical reminders of your unborn child to help you cope with the pain and sting of loss. If you both are not careful you could cause unnecessary tension because of your unwillingness to see grief from the other person's perspective.

A common underlying theme you will continuously discover throughout this book is there is no right or wrong way to grieve. It's imperative that you, as a couple, truly internalize this concept and understand loss drums up a gamut of emotions, feelings, and opinions on how to productively move forward once you've experience the devastation of pregnancy loss. I want to remind you to keep the lines of communication open with your spouse/partner, so that you know where each of you stands as it pertains to your personal grief journeys. Don't be afraid to ask each other what each of you can do to help one another cope and move forward in a healthy manner.

As the mother and physical vessel that carries the baby, it is easy to get bogged down by the weight of our own grief that we dismiss our husbands/partners grief experiences. Just because they can't physically carry the baby doesn't mean that our male counterparts don't feel the deep sting and complete devastation of grief. To further drive home the point how differently men grieve in the face of loss, here is my husband Derrek's account of how the loss of our precious angel DJ affected him as the dad. You may notice some very distinctive differences, how grief was handled from his personal interpretation of our loss, versus how I internalized grief, as DJ's mother, in the previous chapter (Chapter 8: Dealing with Grief (Her Story) page 112). But you may also see some parallels in his account of the tragic events. Nonetheless, this is his personal truth on how he was able to endure DJ's loss and move forward as the head of our household.

*Where it all began*

One day, out of the blue, my wife informed me that she thought she might be pregnant. To assure ourselves that her assumption was true, we bought an at-home pregnancy kit from our local grocery store. Later that evening, my wife took the pregnancy test that came in a box of two. The tests were supposed to display two lines if she was pregnant and one line if she wasn't. The first test we took, showed one clear defined line and another line that was faint. After seeing the faint line, I wasn't one hundred percent sure if my wife was indeed pregnant. So, I asked her to take the second test to see if we got the same results. And we did…one solid line plus a very faint line. I still wasn't certain she was pregnant. So, I asked her to make a doctor's appointment to confirm if the tests she took at home were accurate.

The day of my wife's appointment, it was confirmed Baby Anderson was on the way. The doctor told her that the projected due date was April 7th, which was three days before my birthday. My initial reaction was excitement, as it is for most people, when they find out they are expecting. The news of an addition to your family is usually a joyful occasion, especially for first time parents…like us.

After confirming Baby Anderson was on the way, we knew that life was going to change forever. We would no longer be just husband and wife, but soon we would proudly boast the titles of mommy and daddy. We knew that this would come with big responsibilities as we would now have a little human who was dependent on us…FOR EVERYTHING. That thought was a little scary for us at first, more so with Alishia, but at the end of the day, we knew that we had each other, and we would be able to handle the responsibilities of having a child join our family dynamic.

Early on during the pregnancy, I had a feeling that we were having a boy. I honestly, positively knew, for a fact, that we were having a boy …. no questions asked. As the time drew near for us to find out the gender of the baby, Alishia made me slightly question my certainty of having a son. My confidence decreased slightly from one hundred percent to a solid ninety-five percent. The reality was that the baby would have a fifty-fifty chance of being a boy or a girl. Honestly, I felt like a lot of men, wanting and praying that my first-born child would be a boy. I think we, as men, just want a mini version of ourselves. Someone we can pass our namesake to, to keep our legacy going when we are no longer on this Earth. So, hoping Baby Anderson was a boy, as a father, wasn't too far-fetched in my mind.

The day finally arrived when we would find out our baby's sex. On this day, the nerves kicked in a little for me as I was going to find out if my hunch of having a baby boy was going to come true or if I was just holding on to false hope of having a little mini me. The sonographer started the ultrasound in typical fashion, taking measurements of the head and various body parts. Then came the big gender reveal. The sonographer told us to look at the screen and see if we could tell what we were going to have. In a lot of instances with the ultrasound, I didn't know what I was looking at most of the time, except for the super obvious body parts i.e. the head, arms, legs etc. But when I saw the image of the groin region, I felt like I was looking at my little man's third leg, but then I questioned myself and thought maybe I was just looking at some other miscellaneous body part. The sonographer finally confirmed my hunch, announcing that we officially had a son on the way!

### *My initial reaction to loss*

As the pregnancy progressed, we came up to our normal twenty-eight-week prenatal appointment, which would include another ultrasound. It was the first time we would see our son on the screen after our twenty-week gender reveal ultrasound. Going into this appointment, my wife and I were excited to see our son again on the big screen at the doctor's office. As we waited in the lobby of the doctor's office, and then waited in the ultrasound room where the sonographer was preparing for the appointment, there were a lot of great emotions flowing between Alishia and I in that instant.

When the sonographer started the ultrasound, the first thing she told us was that there was less fluid in the womb than there should be. At the time, we didn't know exactly what that meant, how that happened, or how we could fix it. We figured once we talked with the doctor after the ultrasound that she would help explain all of this and what we needed to do going forward to correct the issue. As the sonographer proceeded with the ultrasound, she measured the first body part, his head. I saw in the corner of the screen that his head measured smaller than what it should have been for a twenty-eight-week-old baby. It only measured at twenty-four weeks. At the time, I knew my wife didn't notice this detail, so I didn't say anything about it, in order to keep her calm during the remainder of the ultrasound. When the sonographer moved onto the second body part, it also measured smaller than what it was supposed to be. All of this was playing out in front of me, but I just figured that our son was developing slower than other normal babies and that it would all work itself out. However, I was still slightly concerned about the fluid levels in the womb being lower than what they should have been.

Then the sonographer moved on to his heart. At the time, we didn't know what she was going to be looking at next, nor did we know it was the heart when she first put the image on the screen. After looking at the image for a few seconds the sonographer pretty much rushed out the room and said that she needed to go and speak with the doctor. Alishia and I said okay but were left puzzled in the ultrasound room, wondering what truly was happening. A few minutes later, the sonographer came back into the room, cleaned the cold jelly from Alishia's tummy, and said we needed to go across the hall to another room to speak to our doctor. With the abrupt conclusion of the ultrasound, we knew something was up, but I told Alishia we would just have to wait to talk with the doctor to see exactly what was going on with our son.

Once we made it to the other room, it didn't take long for the doctor to join us. But this time, instead of one doctor greeting us, two doctors came into the room, which was very unusual. When the doctors entered and got situated, one began speaking. She very gingerly told us that during the ultrasound, the sonographer could not detect our son's heartbeat and that the sonographer legally could not tell us this information during the ultrasound. Hearing the doctor reveal this devastating information was a crushing blow we did not foresee; especially at a routine, twenty-eight-week prenatal appointment. My heart immediately dropped upon hearing the doctor's words, and I knew Alishia's had dropped as well. This was the most devastating news I ever received in my life.

While Alishia broke down into tears immediately, I knew I had to stay strong for the both of us. Being the engineer that I am, I wanted to find some resolve in the situation. I asked the doctors what our next move should be? The first doctor informed us that we needed to go to the hospital to begin the process of delivering our son. This is when we found out why the second doctor was in the room. She was going to be the doctor on call and the doctor who would be at the hospital the weekend we would be there, to help deliver our son. They asked us when we would like to go to the hospital to jumpstart the delivery process, so that they could have a room prepared for us. Our prenatal appointment was on a Friday, but we needed time to process the bombshell the doctors dropped on us that tragic afternoon. We knew the sooner we delivered the baby, the better from a health and mental health standpoint for my wife and me. Therefore, we decided to go to the hospital the following day, which was a Saturday. They asked that we be at the hospital promptly by eight in the morning, so they could begin inducing my wife's labor.

We were deeply saddened and still in disbelief from the news we received at the doctor's office earlier that day when we arrived home. That evening, we cried together, we cuddled on the couch together, and admittedly we questioned God together. So many questions arose from our tragedy like: *Why us? How did this happen? When did DJ pass? What did we do wrong for this to happen? What could we have done differently? What would he have sounded like? What were his likes/dislikes going to be?* And many more questions just like these that we would never get to know the answers to. Amid our shock and sadness, we knew that we had to tell immediate family about the disastrous news we received, which made a tough situation even tougher to process. I had the daunting task of contacting our immediate families to let them know the news. Alishia was not up to talking about it and truthfully, neither was I, but as the head of the house, I knew I had to stand strong in the gap for my wife.

The next morning, we arrived at the Women's Center in the hospital at 8 a.m. as scheduled and checked in at the front desk. It was a sad and awkward feeling for us being in the lobby where we saw other people's relatives waiting in anticipation to see the new additions to their families, while we were heading in to deliver our deceased baby. The silver lining is that we didn't have to endure that awkwardness of waiting in the lobby too long as we were shown to our room relatively fast, because our room was already prepared for us prior to our arrival.

Once we made it to the room, my wife changed into her hospital gown. The nurse explained to us what was going to take place during our hospital stay as well as informed us on some decisions we were going to have to make as the parents of a deceased child. The first question of many we were asked, was if we wanted a funeral and traditional burial of DJ's tiny corpse or would we want to cremate him? We didn't have an answer at that moment, so the nurse stuck a pin in that conversation and said she would revisit it later that day.

Another decision the nurse wanted us to make, in that instant, was deciding after delivery, would we want to see DJ or not. This was a tough decision. We quickly had to weigh the pros and cons of seeing or not seeing the baby. We felt that if we saw him it would just tear us both down emotionally all over again compared to if we did not see him at all. But on the flip side, if we did not see him at that moment, we would never get another opportunity to see him again. After careful consideration, we both agreed that it would be best to see him after delivery because if we didn't we would always regret not seeing him, living in a constant state of wonder.

After three days in the hospital, my wife finally gave birth to our son DJ. For seven months, leading up to that point, we wondered what and who DJ would look like. We unfortunately found out twelve weeks prematurely. He was a tiny, precious miracle, even though he was born a sleeping angel. The nurse measured him at twelve inches and weighed him in at about one and a half pounds. The first thing that I noticed about his appearance, was how delicate his skin looked. Another thing I observed, was the fact that he looked the spitting image of me when I sleep, with his eyes closed and mouth wide open. Even though my son was not born alive, I still felt like a proud dad when I first laid eyes on him and no one could take that special moment away from me.

Immediately after the delivery of DJ, our nurse captured pictures of him as well as pictures with all three of us as a family on our iPhones for personal keepsakes of our son. She also said we could spend as much time as we wanted with DJ as a family. Being allowed the precious time to bond with my son from the nursing staff gave me a great gush of gratitude. It showed me that the hospital understood the magnitude of the time we spent with DJ. They simply understood that we would NEVER get this moment back and allowed us to take as much time as we needed with our stillborn child. To this day, I do not remember how much time we spent with DJ. I'm not quite sure if it was thirty minutes or three hours, all I know is that I was extremely content with my son in that moment and it is time spent I will never forget. It is worthy to note that the hospital also gifted us a professional photoshoot of DJ to have as a memento as well as other special keepsakes for us to remember DJ by. To this day, I still feel gypped by my wife for trying her best to get all dolled up (as dolled up as she could be being in a hospital gown) for the photos without letting me know to get "dolled" up too for the family photos we took. I guess that is just the blogger in her. But nonetheless, the pictures taken that day were one-of-a-kind photos of DJ I will forever cherish.

As the time winded down with DJ, we realized we would never get a chance to see him again in person. The happiness that filled us throughout the day from spending time with our son slowly transitioned into sadness all over again. When Alishia and I finally called the nurse to take DJ, his body was getting colder, and stiffer, and he was slowly changing colors, so we figured it was finally time to say our goodbyes. As the nurse rolled DJ away, my heart felt like it had been ripped out of my chest and stomped on. It was a heartbreaking scene for my wife and me. But reflecting, since a little over a year has passed, I really enjoyed the precious time I got to spend with my baby boy DJ that day. I will continue to treasure the special time we got to bond as father and son for the first and last time, forever!

### Grief from a man's perspective

Dealing with the grief of your lost child is hard, but men go through a similar grieving process with the loss of any family member that is very close. For men, the grieving process is much different than it is for women. Typically, society tells men to be the strong rock for our families. Our mindsets are to naturally stay strong as we do not want to seem weak. And from not wanting to be perceived as "weak," it makes grieving as a man that much harder for us. Therefore, men often deal with grief alone and away from family, friends, and most of all, away from society. It is a very isolating time in a man's life.

This isolation is triggered from the terror of being humiliated by society or anyone when we are in such a vulnerable and delicate state. Men are fearful of getting their man-card revoked for showing too many emotions or weakness. To avoid getting our man-card pulled, we typically deal with grief in seclusion, so we can sort through our grief without judgment. However, there are some men who just want to avoid grief all together and act as if nothing ever happened. Personally, I don't think this is the best option, but to each his own. Isolation is a symptom of grief I encountered, while other men's symptoms of grief include substance abuse, anger, or just being very irritable.

During my grieving process, I wanted to be active to help escape and get my mind off the loss. So, I played video games, went to the gym for some quick workouts, and after about a week removed from the loss, went back to work to try to regain normalcy again. I'm not sure if that was the best way to deal with my grief, but it helped me cope with my tragic loss. Do what you need to do to help blow off steam.

Also, through the process to help get rid of some steam/anger, I felt like I needed a thrill. I remember one time in particular, *the morning Alishia was scheduled to deliver DJ*, I woke up super early (before heading to the hospital at 8 a.m.) and quenched my need for thrill by doing about 120 miles per hour on the freeway in my car. I know that it wasn't the smartest thing to do in the world, but at the time, I didn't care that much. The only little bit of care in me I had, was that if I got pulled over going 120 miles per hour, I would probably go to jail and my already fragile wife would have had to go through delivering our sleeping angel by herself. If the former would have happened, not physically being there for my wife would have crushed me even more during the process. So thankfully, I did not run across any cops during my thrill-seeking process.

I know that not every man handles grieving the loss of their child in the same manner. Instead of wanting to be active or being a thrill seeker, some men may want to talk it out with someone they trust, or a counselor or psychiatrist. But for me, I personally didn't want to talk about it much, especially to a person who had not gone through something similar. So, being active was the best way for me to cope with MY grief.

### Helping my spouse deal with grief while fighting my own grief battle

Throughout our stillbirth journey, my wife had a difficult time processing the loss of our son. And admittedly, a much tougher time than I. Being that I adopted the role of the strong spouse, I could carry her load and mine. I felt if I showed too much sadness, depression, misery, etc., it would take longer for my wife to heal from this tragedy. Therefore, I was the person she leaned on through her tough times. This started from day one, when we heard the tragic news in the doctor's office. Below are some of the ways I helped my wife cope with her grief:

- *Let Her Cry* – I helped my spouse deal with her grief by offering my shoulder for her to cry on. I knew by being there for her in this way, allowing her to let the tears flow and emotionally expose her authentic grief, it would help her move along in her grieving process.
- *Try to Shift or Eradicate Blame* – Immediately after hearing the news, my wife blamed herself for the loss of DJ. She felt she had done something to cause his death; but I knew that was not the case. I tried my best to help her shift her perspective, so she could eventually eradicate blaming herself all together. I did not want her to feel guilty or carry the weight for the loss of our child on her shoulders.
- *Let Her Know That God Has a Plan* – In an effort to help my wife shift or rid herself of blame, I repeatedly told her, God was putting us through this ordeal for a reason and that we would understand its purpose in due time. I let her know God had a plan for our family even through our loss. I also added the perspective that maybe God was putting us through this to aid someone else down the road. Maybe this book was the reason why....to help spread the word on the taboo topic of child loss through stillbirth and encourage someone on this similar journey not to give up hope, no matter how hard grief tries to weigh you down.

- *Prayer* – I prayed to God, often asking for help and guidance to get us through this tough time. But more specifically, I asked God to help my wife as she was having a tough time adjusting to our new reality. I knew if all else failed, prayer would help on our journey of healing. **Spoiler Alert**: Prayer was ultimately one of the major keys that unlocked the door of healing for my wife and me. So, don't be afraid to use prayer as a tool for your healing.

- *Give Her Space* – Throughout my wife's grieving process, I tried to give her as much space as possible, so she could sort out her grief in her own timing. I think having space in general is vital in the grieving process. Granted, I was always one call away. You want to offer enough space, so your partner doesn't feel like you are suffocating them, but you also don't want too much space in where your spouse feels neglected. There is a fine line to find the balance in providing your significant other "space." Just be attentive so you can decipher when they truly need space or when they are truly crying out for help; even if they seem like they may be pushing you away on the surface.

- *Seek Professional Help* – A couple of months after our loss, I noticed my wife was still struggling to cope with our loss. After observing her grief patterns and feeling like my help wasn't enough to sustain her, I recommended she seek professional help to assist her on her grief journey, along with my continued support. Through some research, she came across ten free counseling sessions offered through the Counseling and Psychological Services Department at the university she was attending at the time. It was a total godsend because not only was she able to get the additional help she needed to sort through her pain of loss, she wound up getting ten counseling sessions totally **FREE of charge** through the university from funding allocated from her tuition to student life (if you know me, you know this was music to my ears because my motto is *"you can't beat a discount or getting something for free"*)!!!

- *Shield Her from The Outside World* – To help my wife cope with the loss of our son and properly grieve, I stepped up and intercepted phone calls from friends and family and placed calls to provide updates on our status. I knew in her very fragile state that she could not muster up enough energy to receive calls, so I volunteered to play the "family secretary." By simply taking calls on behalf of my wife and I, it allowed my wife to truly focus on her personal recovery without having to drudge up every detail about the loss of DJ.

- ***Just be a loving husband/partner*** – Throughout our entire ordeal, I just tried to be a loving husband to help my wife through a rough patch. I made sure that I was by her side when she needed me, and I made sure to disappear when she wanted to be alone. I planned trips to help get her mind off the tragedy, I paid for her to take some days of self-care i.e. setting up a massage at a spa or paying for her to get a manicure and pedicure, and I simply spent time with her, if she was up for it. You don't necessarily have to spend money to be a loving partner, you just have to offer yourself and your time.

- ***Don't underestimate the power of date night*** – Lastly, with everything being flipped upside down in your world the best thing to do is to cling to your spouse or partner in this difficult time. Be sure to get some alone time with your partner so that you can strengthen your bond. Dress up nice. Go to your favorite restaurant. Go see a movie. Take a stroll in the park. Go out for ice cream. Take a trip. Whatever you and your spouse like to do; set a time and date, and go have fun doing just that. It will bring you both closer together and allow you time to escape your reality for a short period of time.

With all this weight laying heavy on me from being the man of the household and the rock for my family, I had to dig a little deeper and remain fueled with positivity, faith, and all around good vibes to help maintain strength for my wife and I through the trying times. I didn't mind being the burden bearer because of the love I have for my wife and the love I have for my deceased son. I wouldn't trade this experience for the world, because it helped me "man up" to higher levels and it brought my wife and me even closer together. But, I'd be remiss not to mention I wish I didn't have to lose my son in the process of gaining a lesson in mental fortitude.

### *Things I will miss most about my son*

My son was going to be my junior. He was named after me, Derrek Jerrell Anderson, Jr. So, I was looking forward to seeing how much my mini me would have turned out to be like daddy. Because of his untimely death, I will never get to know exactly how much he would've followed in my footsteps. I will never know how he would have sounded when he cried or talked. I will never know what his favorite foods would have been, nor will I ever know what would have been his favorite subjects in school. I will never know what his favorite sports would have been or if he would have liked sports at all. Nor will I ever know ... do you see where I'm going with this?

The list can go on and on indefinitely. I will never get to know the type of boy or man he would've grown to be and that is something that will always haunt me and make me wonder. I will never be able to get a definitive answer to my questions until we meet again one day in heaven but, I can rest my faith in knowing that while I was robbed of my time on Earth with DJ, I will one day reconnect with him in heaven which offers me comfort. One day, in eternity, I hope I will be able to get my questions answered, until then I will long in anticipation to see my son's face again.

On the other hand, DJ was here physically in my wife's womb for a short amount of time in the grand scheme of things. While his body is no longer here with us physically, his spirit and legacy live on through my wife and me. I will always cherish DJ forever and reminisce often about the brief time we had together here on Earth. He was a very tiny baby, which is understandable since he only completed about seven gestational months in my wife's womb. Even though he was tiny in frame, all his major parts i.e. his head, chest, arms, legs, feet, toes, etc., were intact. DJ looked like a normal baby for his size and that is one thing I'm truly grateful of, in the midst of him losing his life.

The thing I will miss most about DJ, is seeing him in general. But more specifically seeing his little feet and hands as they were the most precious little things. I will miss touching his very delicate skin. I will miss seeing him with his eyes closed and mouth wide open as he looked like a mirror image of me when I sleep, according to my wife. I will miss being able to hold his light and fragile body. I will miss being able to talk to him. I will miss spending family time as a trio with him, my wife, and me. I will miss being a father to him. I will miss seeing him grow from a newborn into a toddler, adolescent, teenager, then adult. There are so many other things that I will miss that I do not have words for. But I will always miss him! I will always remember him! I will always love him! And he will always be my son! No one can take that away from me.

*On the other side of grief (picking up the pieces and creating a new normal)*

After going through a loss, there is a point in time where grief settles, and you begin to settle into your new normal. This new normal can be very tough to adjust to at first, but each minute that passes, each hour that passes, each day that passes, your new routine gets easier and becomes a part of the new YOU. After our loss, our new normal included several different things. The first part of our new normal was growing closer to each other as a young couple. I feel that going through adversity and tragedy can end up two ways; either it can break you or it can make you stronger. For us, I feel like it ultimately made each of us individually stronger, and it made our relationship stronger as a couple.

From the loss, I also feel that our non-verbal and verbal communication improved as well. I think this was done by taking cues from my wife and learning when to cling to one another, and when to offer each other space. When you put in the effort to truly be there for your partner, when they need a shoulder to lean on or give them the space they need when they need to cool off, it makes a world of difference and allows you to connect on a much deeper level.

Lastly, don't being afraid to face your fears from the tragedy you just faced head on. In our case, we didn't let the tragic loss of our first-born, sleeping angel, DJ, stifle us from dreaming about the possibility of one day conceiving a second child. We didn't let the fear of our past with the loss of our child dictate the joy and happiness that the future would bring. By adopting this mindset, we have been able to pick up the scattered remnants of our loss and have even experienced pockets of sunshine after the storm.

### *Conclusion of dealing with grief (his story)*

I know, in life, we all go through our ups and downs, and we have our blessings and misfortunes. But through it all, life goes on, as time waits for no man. Since this is the case, I feel we all need to enjoy life the best that we can, while we can. Even though we experienced the devastating loss of our child, I still tried to have a positive outlook on the situation. I believed if I somehow kept a positive outlook on the unfortunate occurrences, later in the future, it would be beneficial for me or for someone else. I truly believe that because we tried to keep a positive outlook on the situation, it helped us navigate our grief better. Even though we were experiencing a type of loss that NO ONE is truly ready for, we were able to use our spiritual eyes to eventually see the bigger plan God had in store for our lives materialize because of how we coupled our grief with our belief and total faith in Him.

First, it led my wife to wanting to write this book in hopes that it would help someone else identify and tackle their own personal grief after child loss. It has also propelled my wife into shedding light into the dark crevices of pregnancy child loss (via stillbirth). I truly applaud and admire my wife in her efforts to spread the word about such a taboo subject. As my wife mentioned before, I am more of a closed book. I like to keep things to myself or share personal details about my life only in my very tightknit circle composed of my immediate family and a few close friends. My wife, on the other hand, is more of an open book, sharing her experiences with the world. Through her transparency, she is allowing God to use her gift of writing, sharing, and connecting with others to educate a multitude of people on grief and child loss.

Secondly, I feel that God taught me a lot personally through the whole ordeal of loss and grew me more as a person and as a man. As I look back on the twenty-eight weeks when my wife was pregnant with DJ, I realized I shared with her a lot of things *I wanted* (I only wanted a son) and certain things *I didn't want* (how I did not want a daughter) for my first child. I also realized that I complained about little stuff like not wanting to turn my office into a nursery. But once DJ passed I thought to myself, why was I being so selfish and somewhat ungrateful? I had this precious gift that God was blessing us with and I just couldn't be one hundred percent appreciative about the whole situation. I've come to the realization that God wanted to use me losing a child to grow me. I am grateful that God loved me enough to use this tough situation to make me a more mature man. From my experience of losing DJ, I was careful not to complain about anything and I allowed myself to open my [spiritual] eyes and truly enjoy the everyday blessings that God surrounded us with that I normally missed in my state of selfish reflection.

Grief will always be hard, no matter who you've lost. And going through the grief process is different for each individual (especially men who often suffer in silence). Nonetheless, I am here to say that you can make it through the grief process by taking it one day at a time. But I do want to challenge you to try and turn your negative situation into a positive one. In my case, I told myself God allowed us to go through our situation to build a testimony, one that would allow us to help someone down the road and that seemed to help me focus on my healing during my grief journey. I hope you find the same solace and new-found purpose I found. Good luck! I know you can do it – *from one sleeping angel survivor father to another.*

# Chapter 10

## Keep Going

*"But as for you, be strong and courageous,*
*for your work will be rewarded."*
*– 2 Chronicles 15:7 New Living Translation*

Let me let you in on a little secret. Somedays, you will wake up and not think about the loss of your child once. It sounds terrible, but it is the honest truth, especially the further removed you are from the loss of your angel. Somedays the weight of the internal pain will hit you like a ton of bricks…usually when you least expect it. There will be days you are filled with family, fun, and laughter, and other times when you will feel isolated, lonely, and down in the dumps. You will experience extreme highs and detrimental lows throughout your grief journey. You will have days of triumph and then turn around and experience days of pain. But rest assured, it all comes with the grief territory. There is no textbook way to deal with or experience grief (unless you are trying to physically harm yourself. If that is the case, please seek out help immediately).

Whatever it is that you do…just KEEP GOING. Don't let the weight of such a crushing experience change the total essence of who you were before you realized you would carry the title of stillbirth survivor. In the famous words of Destiny's Child: ***"I'm a survivor, I'm not gon' give up, I'm not gon' stop, I'm gon' work harder. I'm a survivor, I'm gonna make it, I will survive, keep on surviving!"*** In other words, I will keep going. I will keep moving forward. I will pick up the remaining pieces and do what I need to do to live my life with purpose, passion, and in a way, that will honor my fallen angel. Like Dory said in Finding Nemo, ***"just keep swimming."*** Swim through the waves of despair. Swim through the tough moments and swim until you feel your journey take a turn for the best.

Trust me when I say, things will get better. The deep despair you feel will eventually lighten its load. Your grief passenger that has demanded to drive will quietly move into the passenger seat, and later take a back seat to the rest of your life. You will be able to look back on your situation with a fresh pair of eyes and see the hidden gems that you missed while you were stifled in a state of grief.

Until you see the light at the end of the tunnel, just keep moving. If you can't run toward healing, jog. If you can't jog, walk. If you can't walk toward healing, crawl. If you can't crawl, scoot. Whatever you do, just keep going. Don't stop moving. It may seem like you can't make it, but I'm here to encourage you and let you know **YOU CAN MAKE IT**. You may be on day one of your journey, but just know even when you feel like you can't go on, you will make it!

The key to defeating the heaviness of baby loss is constant movement toward healing. You don't have to go at a record-breaking pace, just stay in your lane, exercise your faith, keep your eyes on the faint light at the end of the tunnel, and take a step. God is right there with you. He is guiding you on the days you need a guide. He will pick you up and carry you on the days you feel like you cannot go on. He will prop you up on the days you feel like you can no longer stand. When it is all said and done, you will be rewarded for your tenacity, your strength, even your weakness, and your ability to keep going in spite of.

# Chapter 11

## Discovering Your New Normal

*"And though you started with little,
you will end with much."*
- **Job 8:7** *New Living Translation*

From the moment you hear those dreaded words…**"we couldn't locate a heartbeat,"** your life irrevocably changes forever! All the hopes and dreams you fanaticized about your baby suddenly disappear like a magic trick gone awry. Those words have a sting like no other. You never think to cherish the sound coming from the Fetal Doppler each time the doctor locates the heartbeat during a visit. But boy, do I wish I could just hear the thumping sound of my son's racing heart just one more time. When I look back on my pregnancy those are the tiny miracles I took for granted as I awaited my son's arrival in gestational bliss. It never even crossed my mind that we would not make it across the finish line with a handsome, healthy, breathing bundle of joy. I just assumed that once I made it past the first trimester, I was home free. Instead, we were left to pick up the pieces of our shattered hearts and start life anew without the physical presence of our little prince charming.

Many people will offer their condolences, kind words, words of encouragement, gifts, and even mementos to help you try to "get over" the loss of your child. But the truth is, you will NEVER "get over" losing your child, no matter if he/she was your first or twentieth. The permanent nature of losing someone you will never get a chance to meet again in this lifetime is a tough pill to swallow. When people say things like *"It was God's will,"* or *"You can try for another baby"* they don't seem to realize that you didn't lose your keys or your favorite shirt; you lost a human being, one you helped to create. You lost hearing them cry for the first time, you lost changing their diaper, you lost bath time, you lost story time before bed, you lost breast or bottle feeding, you lost dressing them in your favorite outfit, you lost bonding time, you lost first words, first steps, the first day of school, their first "ouchie," and their first crushes. When your baby dies, so does your future with your baby and all the firsts of your life and theirs. People don't realize that when they say... *"well you can try for another baby"* that is an insult not a complement. The funny thing is, I was content with the baby I had. I didn't want another baby. I would have done just fine with DJ. Instead, I was forced to start over as you will be.

Discovering your new normal can feel daunting at times. It can feel unfair. It can feel uncomfortable. It can feel strange. It can feel unfamiliar. It can make you feel lost. But just remember, there is no manual you must follow when living out your new normal. If you lose your baby and don't want to talk about him or her ever again, then that is your prerogative. If you lose your child and you want to share your story with everyone you meet, that is your prerogative also. You are the author of this chapter of grief and loss in your life. Don't let anyone tell you differently. What works for some, may not work for others as you try to cope with your new reality the best way you see fit. For my husband and I, our new normal is acknowledging that our son indeed was here on this Earth and keeping his legacy, spirit, and presence alive through tireless efforts. Additionally, we strive to spread the word about our triumphs, struggles, grief, contentment and so much more that comes along with being the parents of a stillborn child. As time moves further and further away from when our son was born, it takes more of a strategic effort to keep his memory burning on the forefront of our minds and the minds of others. There are some things you must keep in mind when you are trying to adjust to your new normal.

### *Your lens on life may drastically change.*

When you gleefully wait on the anticipated arrival of your son or daughter and realize at some point you will no longer receive your happy ending, it takes some major physical, mental, emotional, and even spiritual adjustments. After losing DJ a house of two suddenly felt empty and cold. Life just didn't seem the same. At first, colors no longer seemed as bright, sounds didn't seem as clear, and tastes didn't seem as defined. When we first lost our son, it felt as if I was walking around in the twilight zone, aimlessly. Although I had my soul and mind anchored in Christ Jesus, it did not negate the fact that I was hurting. I was grieving. My life was like a ship tossed and tussled by the stormy seas, which wrecked. I still feel this pain daily but through this process of sadness, loneliness, isolation, sorrow, etc., I've been able to adjust my lens and perspective on this life I live.

I decided I would not let my baby die in vain. I would use my platform and firsthand experience to help others stand boldly in the face of stillbirth (miscarriage, neonatal death, baby or infant loss). No longer did I want women, men, mothers, fathers, sisters, brothers, grandparents and extended family members, or even family friends to have to hide behind the stigma of losing a child. I wanted to stand boldly in my new normal, toting my badge of childlessness with my head held high. I wanted to use my platform to help people realize that their children were blessings from God. Even if their precious angel was stripped away from this side of life, it didn't take away the fact their baby's life was just as valuable.

I decided I would stand up and make my son proud by using his life, his death, and his legacy to build a megaphone to speak about the mountain peaks and the valleys of losing a child. By no means am I an expert. I am simply a grieving mother doing the best I can to move forward in life without becoming a bag lady, carrying around luggage filled with anger, bitterness, disappointment, envy, jealousy and other traits unbecoming of whom I strive to be. If I can be totally candid, these feelings do surface here and there but when they do arrive, I acknowledge their arrival and pledge to myself and them that they cannot stay long.

### *You have a choice about how you will handle your grief*

Through my grieving process, I've noticed I have a personal choice about how I will let my situation affect me, my mood, and ultimately my day. If all I do is focus on the loss of my son, I am missing the beauty that occurred while he was alive. I am missing out on the joy he brought, to not only my husband and myself, but to countless others. I am missing out on the anticipation and longing we experienced waiting for his arrival. I am missing out on the abundance of love that was bestowed upon us across the country when we announced our little blessing to our family and friends.

Through this grieving process, I vowed to myself I would not let my grief overshadow my pledge to keep my son's legacy alive. I am raw and honest about sharing my grieving emotions with others. Some days, I am not fine. I feel as if the world is crashing down on me and I miss my son with every fiber of my being. On other days, I marvel in awe at the tiny creation my husband and I were so blessed to create and hold in our arms.

You are the captain of your grieving ship. Whatever you want to get out of it, you have the authority to do so. While I simply wanted to use my situation to bring awareness to losing a child, I've gained much more in the process. I've gained a deeper spiritual connection with my creator, I've gained a deeper empathy for those who are going through life's hardships, and I've gained a deeper understanding of what true love feels like. Through this journey, just remember you have a choice on how you will welcome in your grief. Will you fight off your grief like a bandit in the night or will you accept your grief has a purpose? The choice is truly up to you. Whichever method of healing you choose, stand shamelessly in it!

*After loss, you will begin to notice and appreciate things more*

It's funny how the school of life teaches us to be grateful. While our society harps on consumerism, buying and accumulating more stuff, having the latest, greatest clothing, electronics, music, house, car, education, career, etc., this hardship of losing my son taught me to appreciate all things; the big and the small, the heartache, the pain, the sunshine, the rain. It taught me to truly look around and within to reflect on all the blessings I overlooked in the hustle and bustle of going about my daily routine.

I make it a point to internalize and express all the things I am grateful for. Every night before bed, I write in my journal. I have made it a practice, even on those days when I find myself down in the dumps, to write three things I'm grateful for. You'd be surprised how much you have to be thankful for in the midst of losing your child. It is an exercise I incorporate into my daily routine, to always keep in mind the number of blessings that are bestowed upon me daily. The mere fact that I have a heartbeat, or eyesight, or hearing the birds chirping in the morning, or seeing the sun rise and set, or hearing the wind whistle a tune, or seeing a unique light show when lighting strikes the sky accompanied by a thunderous soundtrack, is a blessing in and of itself.

There are so many things we can be thankful for but it all depends on our mindset. I can walk around mad at the world that my son out of all the babies in the world had to be one of 26,000 annually in the United States to lose his life. But I choose not to examine my personal situation in that manner. I choose to appreciate the life he *did* live. I choose to honor the fact that I was with him his entire journey of passing through Earth. I choose to delight in the fact that I am the mother to an important angel…as are all of you reading this book! So, it seems that even through my tragedy, I've unlocked an unlimited supply of gratefulness, optimism, and thanksgiving. I dare you to give it a try.

### *Loss gives you the opportunity to put life into perspective and take hold of it*

Losing DJ taught me one major life lesson. It taught me that life is fleeting. Life is not promised. While these phrases are cliché, their meanings hold true. Life is ever fleeting. The day we are born puts us one step closer to death. But what you do with your time on Earth is up to you. You can use your borrowed time to complain, mope, be buried in sadness, spew hate, be disrespectful, sing "woe is me" or you can use the one life you were given to hold your head high, spread love and positivity, be a light in a dark place, build strong relationships with God, your spouse/companion, and your children, to chase after and accomplish your dreams, to bring about change in the world and much more. I want to do the latter. After seeing a firm example of life not being promised through the passing of my son, I realized I must not waste the one life I've been given. I have to use it to be a light, to be an example of triumph in spite of heartache, to go after my dreams, to dream big, dream in color, and dream often, to trust the process, to experience failure and learn the proper lessons from it, and to shoot for the moon, the sun, and even the stars. All I'm saying is that life is worth living to the fullest. When it is all said and done, I want God to call me home and say, "well done my good and faithful servant." I want my son to look down from heaven and exclaim to all the other angel babies, "that's my mom, which one is yours?" in a proud manner! Don't let life pass you by with the loss of your angel. Pick up the mantel and take life by the horns. Use your grief and turn it into triumph by keeping your angel's legacy alive in your everyday life. No matter how you make your angel proud, just do something that will positively impact your life and in turn help you continue to move forward.

### *It may take a little time to get acclimated with your old routine*

From the time my son was pronounced dead at the doctor's office, to the time I delivered him and held him in my arms, everything was a whirlwind. There was so much on my mind that I couldn't think about my "normal" life or routine. But once the dust settled, and I got back home, I realized things that were mundane before i.e. straightening up the living room, washing the dishes, doing laundry, making the bed, cooking breakfast, lunch, or dinner, or even rising to go fellowship at church, seemed harder to do. I say this to give you a sense of relief. Don't be hard on yourself if you find it harder than normal to get back into the swing of things. You have to remember you didn't just lose your puppy or $20, you lost your own flesh and blood. You lost someone you assisted in creating. That can truly take a toll on you.

Give yourself the freedom to be human. Don't think you have to be superman or superwoman and jump right back into your daily routine like you never left. Give yourself time to heal and grieve. Allow yourself room to make mistakes. Ask for help when you feel like you can't do simple tasks. You must realize that losing your child isn't just something you bounce back from with ease. Be gracious to yourself and patient with others. This is an on-the-job-learning experience. You will find what works best for you, your spouse and your family. Just do what you can to stay afloat until you hit your groove. If you have to, fake it until you make it!

### *The more time that passes the harder it gets*

I had my son three months early. I was twenty-eight weeks when I delivered him. I experienced a whirlwind of emotions from the moment I found out he had no heartbeat to the time I delivered him. Even though I was in labor for three days, I had a calming peace come over me the instance I saw his face (probably because I prayed for it and God answered my prayer). While in the hospital, I was in a bubble of protection, care, and sympathy. But once I left, I had to face the bitter reality that the real world wasn't so incubated. As time commenced, the realization set in that my son was truly gone. When I approached my due date, the harsh reality that I would not have a baby by my side set in. As I began to see other women who were pregnant around the same time as me or after me deliver healthy babies, the sting of my son's death hit a little harder than usual. Even as I sit and write this book ten months later, I realize that the pain I felt when I first heard there was no heartbeat, is still as prevalent as it was on January 15. They say, "time heals all wounds," but it doesn't really heal the wounds as much as it helps you cope with them better. The wounds will always be there. The scar of losing your child will be worn for the rest of your life, but the puncture of disappointment, despair, heartbreak and more will gradually become a lighter burden to bear.

What I will say, is the more time passes, the harder it is to accept the fact that your child is truly not with you. I find myself thinking about life and how it could, would, or should be if my son was here with me. I wouldn't have to try to start over and try to have another baby. I wouldn't have to turn away from baby commercials that show newborns in their full glory. I wouldn't have to fanaticize about what my son would look like and how he would act at certain developmental stages. I wouldn't be down internally when I see another woman proudly toting her round baby bump or holding her little munchkin in the store. I wouldn't try to guess what my son and I would be doing on a random day in August. Just the little things you are missing out on can be tough to help you find your new normal.

Please be reminded that although your life may contain remnants of what used to be predating your baby loss, your life will never be completely the same again. This is not to sadden you or make you dread what is to come, it is simply to inform you that you may have to adjust to the new frontier laid before you. Use this time of reconstruction and discovery to rebuild a new normal that you can be proud of. Use this time to focus inward so you can be the best version of yourself for your partner, children, family and friends, but most importantly, yourself!

# Chapter 12

## Seeking Help

*"The way of a fool is right in his own eyes,
but a wise man seeks counsel."*
– **Proverbs 12:15** *New American Standard Bible*

When I first left the hospital, I had my mom and husband with me for a few days. We all reflected on the time we had had in the hospital: with me going into labor, seeing DJ, then saying goodbye to him all in the same day. I cried slightly thinking of the little munchkin I had to leave behind, but overall, I did fairly well emotionally after losing such a big piece of my life. But once my mother left, my husband went back to work, and the dust began to settle, my emotions went totally haywire. The further removed I got from my son's official birthdate (January 18, 2016) the more emotional I became. I would ease through the day, going about my old routine: house chores, school work, organizational activities, projects, church ministry obligations and then I would lay down at the end of the day and bawl my eyes out for hours on end. I felt like I was riding a never-ending, grief-filled merry-go-round. It was the same scenario over and over and over again for months.

I found it interesting how I was able to compartmentalize my day to do what I had to do and some days I was even able to have a smile on my face and enjoy the things that I was doing. But after a busy day, when my body became still, my mind would race nonstop recounting the events that led up to me saying goodbye to DJ. Like clockwork, the vision of my husband and me sitting in the ultrasound room, excitedly waiting to see our twenty-eight-week-old son on the screen only to be told there is no heartbeat, would occur nightly. From there, my mind would race to the scene when we came home from the doctor's office and my husband and I cried our eyes out, sat in silence, and held each other close as we tried to process our tragic fate. Then my mind would carry me to my hospital experience of being induced, getting an epidural an hour before delivery, feeling pressure in my lower abdomen, the nurses rushing in to tell me my son was crowning, then pushing about five good times before seeing my precious angel for the first time.

My mind would sweetly travel to the intimate moments Derrek and I experienced with DJ and how even the sorrow evoked a strange sense of peace, amazement, and wonder. But my dreams always ended in the ultimate nightmare with us putting our baby in a transferrable incubator for the last time and saying goodbye. What parents should have to say goodbye to their twenty-eight-week-old son? He should've remained inside my belly, cooking for two additional months before I saw his handsome face. I shouldn't have had to plan his cremation. After the last vision of the nurse rolling him out of the room played on the jumbotron of my mind, the waterworks would begin, and I could not shut them off until I cried myself to sleep.

This vision would occur nightly as I tried to peacefully rest. Like clockwork, I would lay down and, starting from the beginning, my mind would go through the events leading up to my husband and I saying goodbye to our child forever, and again the waterworks where I would cry for hours. As the weeks transitioned into months, this same recurring event would occur nightly. While the crying spells didn't last nearly as long, I still wept almost every day. During this time, I was navigating through my new normal by offering transparent commentary through brutally honest journal writing, and by using my fashion blog and various social media platforms to share my true feelings. At the beginning, when we first lost DJ, I received countless text messages, calls, Facebook messages, Instagram posts, etc. But as time moved on, so did the overwhelming outpour of support from people for our situation. I totally get it, people will offer you the cliché "*sorry for your loss*" or "*I'm praying for you*" or "*Your family is in my prayers.*" I know, because I was one of those people. Don't get me wrong, I truly believe people are touched, saddened, and even devastated from the news of your loss, but they have their own daily issues they must confront, so they tend to move on. But when the loss happens to you, it is not something you can just address once then move on. It is a never-ending process of trying to figure out how you pick up and mend the million shattered pieces of your heart.

I remember as time moved further from my son's birthdate, I talked to my husband a lot about missing DJ. I would talk to my mom as well because they were the two people who were in the trenches with me as the situation unfolded. Both always lent a listening ear, but I sometimes felt that they got a little tired talking about the same things over and over. All I could do was talk about DJ because it was one way that I personally dealt with grief. The more I talked about him and sought to explain the situation the more release I felt.

Although it felt good to talk about DJ to my husband and to my mother, I knew it was tough on them as they too were going through their own grieving journeys simultaneously as a dad and grandmother. Many other family members reached out to me and expressed that I could call them anytime if I needed to talk, including my dad, brothers, sisters-in-law, and many more. But I didn't want to be a burden and dump my grief problems on them. So often, when I wanted to truly unload my feelings, I would simply journal them. I would write recklessly, trying to transfer the millions of scattered thoughts in my mind onto the structured lines of my journal. Some days, I would write until my hand hurt. I would write about any and everything. How I was feeling. Things that were said to me that may have been insensitive. Memories about DJ that made me smile. Whatever was on my mind, I would dump it all into my journal, which at the time when I was writing it, felt amazing. But once I was done I would still feel hollow inside. Like something was missing.

After going through the keepsake box my nurse gifted me, I found some information about digital support groups. One of the groups I joined: "Forever Angel Babies Support" was a closed Facebook group of hundreds of moms and dads across the globe that have experienced loss through stillbirth, miscarriage, or infant loss. While it is a terrible way to meet such amazing people (men and women alike join the group) it was very comforting to have people who knew exactly what I was feeling to express my thoughts, fears, worries, sadness, and anger to. Some days, I would just go to the closed Facebook group and read different posts for hours, that grieving mothers and fathers would write. I would sympathize with them and if I felt led to comment, I would. I remember a few times when I wrote posts about what I was feeling, the amount of love and support I received from women, complete strangers, who could identify first-hand what I was going through. While it did not bring my son back, it did help comfort me in some of the most trying times to let me know I was not alone, that I was not crazy, and that I was not silly for having the thoughts I was having.

One time, I recall writing to the group about my six-week, post-partum appointment to follow up with my doctor after having DJ. I remember feeling very anxious about the appointment. I wasn't sure how I would be able to handle the visit emotionally, being at the same doctor's office where six weeks' prior, my son was given his death sentence. I was anxious to sit in a waiting room full of blissful pregnant women and their partners as my husband and I sat empty-handed, wondering why our child wasn't as lucky to make it across the finish line healthy and alive. I was nervous to walk pass the ultrasound room where the fate of my angel was sadly decided with the click of a button. I was petrified to hear what had caused my son's death after the autopsy results were in. Overall, I was just very apprehensive about the entire appointment. I mentioned my anxieties to my husband and he told I should be ok, but that wasn't the answer I was looking for in the moment.

I went to my digital support group and told them my dilemma. They were so understanding. Many women chimed in about their six-week post-partum experience after losing their child. They assured me that I would make it through and not to be hard on myself. They sent me well wishes and told me that I was strong. It is so interesting to me that the well-wishes of total strangers were the most comforting remedy. They didn't know me, and I didn't know them personally, but we had a common bond like no other. Those bonds truly helped me get through some very tough times.

Another ally I found in the mist of my grieving, was a classmate who one month prior to me losing my son, had lost her mother to brain cancer. While we were not experiencing the same type of loss, we found solace in one another on our darkest days. I remember one day, we had just finished class, and my classmate and I were the last two people in the lab. We both were working on an assignment when I asked her how she was holding up. She told me, "some days are better than others." At that exact moment, I knew we were on the same page. We exchanged grief stories for the next hour or so. It was therapeutic and refreshing to have someone who knew what I was going through even though I was suffering the grief of a child and she, as the child, was suffering the grief of losing her mother. We cried, we hugged it out, and we vowed that if either of us needed to talk, we could call or text each other. When I had a grief spell, I would often text her to check on her to see how she was doing. I was thirty at the time, while she was only twenty-two, so I felt like her big sister. I wanted to protect her as much as I could. Our relationship had a deeper connection and blossomed into a true friendship through our connection with grief.

A member at my dad's church also proved to be a beneficial ally I found through my grief process. A few years prior to my incident, she and her husband suffered the loss of their first child through stillbirth. I remember when it happened because my parents, the pastor and first lady of our church, went to visit her and her husband at the hospital after she gave birth to the baby. I remember thinking how sad they lost the baby, but until I was forced to go through the same scenario years later, I really didn't understand the life-altering impact baby loss had on them that tragic day. When I first spoke to Shamika, it seemed as if she was reading an excerpt directly out of my journal. Prior to my incident, I didn't even know what the term stillbirth meant. I had never heard it discussed when speaking about possible pregnancy outcomes. Shamika explained to me that all the things I was feeling were valid. The endless sadness, the tears, the anger, the bitterness, the gratitude, etc., were all emotions that she too experienced. She told me that with time, prayer, faith, and the help and support of her husband she was able to make it through to the other side of grief. She also was a source of inspiration as she explained the story of having her rainbow baby, a son named Quincy. It was refreshing to see a real-life example of what I was going through. To see she made it through the tough times of grief lifted my spirits. To also know that she had a rainbow baby after losing her first was something I too could look forward too. We exchanged numbers, and she told me I could call her anytime I needed to talk or just vent. It is helpful to know that you have the support of someone who has walked a mile in your shoes. It makes the situation more manageable.

Even with all the support from my husband, my parents, my in-laws, my siblings, my friends, my classmates, the digital support group, and much more, I still felt like I wasn't progressing in my grief as I should. I talked with my husband and asked him if I could find a therapist. For me, finding a therapist was a huge step. I had never in my life visited a therapist before. I had no idea what I was looking for, but I thought a therapist would be a great resource to have help me balance my home life and school life (it was my last semester of college…I had a 4.0 GPA and I wanted to ensure I kept that GPA my last semester even though I had just experienced the most tragic event in my life).

At first when I was looking for a therapist, I was searching for one through my insurance. My husband and I were both on the lookout for someone who could help me. Then one day, while I was searching through my university's website, I stumbled upon counseling services offered through my school. As a student, I was able to get ten counseling sessions, free of cost! That was like music to my ears. I could go talk to someone on campus every other week to help me sort through my grief and stay on track with my studies. It was a win-win for me.

I was a nervous wreck my first appointment. I had never been to a counseling office before, so I had no clue what to expect. I filled out some confidentiality forms and answered a questionnaire. I was then escorted to the back and met with a girl who ran through my questionnaire, asking me to explain each answer. For the most part, it was a pleasant conversation. However, she told me she was interning at the office that semester for her Master's. She asked me if I would prefer a more "seasoned" counselor to work out my grief. I told her I thought that would be best. She mentioned there was one person in the office whom she thought I would benefit from and that she would schedule the next appointment with her. I thanked her for her help and willingness to pass me off to someone she thought I could benefit from more and that was the beginning of my counseling journey.

The first day I met Dr. Holly Brown, I was pleasantly surprised at how inviting her personality was. It felt like I could sit and talk with her for hours, considering my sessions were for sixty minutes. My first session, she went over the same questionnaire that the first therapist went over with me, then she asked me why I wanted counseling. I explained to her I had lost my twenty-eight-week-old son about a month or two prior to our first session. She then asked me to tell her the story from the beginning, and that was the start of our therapist – patient relationship. For the next ten weeks, I met with Dr. Holly almost every week. I loved meeting with her because she was an outside party who could objectively see my situation with a fresh pair of eyes. She listened attentively while I poured out my fears, frustrations, emotions and much more without judgement.

She would allow me to cry, vent or ask a multitude of questions to try to help me get to a place where I felt there was some form of closure or resolution. She often gave me little nuggets and tips to help me get through certain situations I was dealing with along my grief journey that truly helped. One was the never ending why. She assured me that when you are grieving, you tend to ask why quite often. She told me there was no harm in asking why, but we shouldn't get caught up in the why because it could be a never-ending spiral into a deep depression. With that, she told me to give myself a time limit to write down all my whys then she said once the time limit was up, come up with answers for the whys that I was satisfied with. Once I was satisfied with the answer, I was to move onto the next why. I did this exercise and it truly helped me realize the answer I chose didn't matter, it didn't change the situation. At the end of the day this was a card life dealt me and I had to figure out how to manage my hand wisely even with my endless source of whys.

My "aha moment" with Dr. Holly came when she helped me realize the fact that emotions are not good or bad they just are. I would tell her how I would get through the day happy, with energy, smiling even, but at night, I would fall apart. She told me when I described "falling apart" I would describe it in such a way that it had a negative connotation. I never realized how "ashamed" I felt for breaking down, crying, or showing weakness. But she assured me that all those emotions were simply a part of grieving. The sadness, the anger, the joy, the gratefulness, the confusion and much more were just feelings. She explained no feelings are better or worse than the other, they just are. That to me was the most profound thing I got from our session. I felt like a caged bird being set free for the first time. It helped me become unashamed of what I was feeling. That was why I was able to become so open about what I was going through on social media. I wasn't afraid to express my vulnerability because all humans are vulnerable with something. I wasn't afraid to express my sadness because we've all been saddened by loss before. I wasn't afraid to express my gratefulness for my son entering my life because I knew there were people out there who could relate. Being able to just live in your emotions and let them pass over you was such a freeing experience. It felt amazing to just be able to let go and let loose. I was able to say that this was just all a part of my own grief journey. Each of us has a grief journey. No one grief journey is identical to the other. You have to navigate the endless maze of grief the best way you know how. Some days, you may feel like you're masterfully navigating your way through grief's challenges while others, may feel like you keep running into the same dead end of despair. No matter where you are, keep going. Don't let the weight of grief paralyze you.

Grief is such a heavy burden to bear. That is why I don't think you should do it alone. Whatever you need to do to find help, whether it's through your spouse, through a close friend, through a support group, through your Pastor or clergy at church, or through a therapist, do it. The end result is that you want to be able to find the necessary assistance and support to help you get through your grief. Eventually, you will be on the other side of grief and can, in turn, help someone else who is just starting off like you once did. It is a never-ending cycle, but grief is something you don't have to do alone. You can create your own tribe to help you get through it!

# Chapter 13

## Carrying On Your Angel's Legacy

*"For we are God's masterpiece.*
*He has created us anew in Christ Jesus,*
*so, we can do the good things*
*he planned for us long ago."*
*– **Ephesians 2:10** New Living Translation*

From the moment, I left the hospital after delivering DJ, I knew my life would not be the same. I wasn't sure how it would change or how drastically it would change, but I knew that it would be different. After gaining some minor relief from the knick-knacks, trinkets, articles of clothing, reading material, and pictures of our son from the hospital, which tremendously helped my husband and I start to heal, I knew I wanted to do something further to carry on my son's legacy while helping other families experiencing pregnancy or infant loss just like we did.

Losing a child is uncharted territory for most. Our society recognizes when a child loses their parents that they are referred to as orphans. When a husband or wife loses their spouse, they are called a widow or widower. But there is no word to pinpoint or describe the devastation of parents who lose a child, besides heartbroken. Although I wouldn't wish this position on any other parents, the loss of a child throughout pregnancy or in a baby's infant stage is far too common and a lot of times unexplainable. The doctors told us DJ was a healthy baby boy when he passed away. Even after countless ultrasounds, a physical exam after he was born, bloodwork, and even an autopsy there was no conclusive evidence they could gather from examining me or him that caused his death (besides the acknowledgement that he stopped growing at twenty-four weeks when he was born at twenty-eight weeks). That unsettling feeling of not knowing how or why my baby's life was cut short is one that haunts me at night sometimes. The insecurity of possibly running into the same fate with a subsequent pregnancy is a huge piece of the puzzle as well.

For my own peace of mind, I knew I wanted to do something that would carry on my son's legacy so that his life would not be in vain. Every chance I get, I try to speak his name, recount his short-lived life here on earth, and remind others that although he is not here physically with us, his spirit and legacy always remains in our hearts. It may be difficult at first to try to come up with a way to honor your child, but I think it is an important step in the healing process. These gestures validate your child's existence and help promote their legacy to you, your family, and to others. There are countless ways you can honor your child's legacy! I'll first start with how my husband and I decided we would honor our son (annually) to commemorate and honor his short-lived life here on this planet.

***#DoGood4DJ***

My son was born on Monday, January 18, 2016…on Martin Luther King Jr. Day at twenty-eight weeks (twelve weeks prior to his scheduled due date). We acknowledge that January 18 is his official birthday, which we have vowed we will celebrate each year, but April 7th still holds a dear place in our hearts and psyche. April 7th was DJ's scheduled due date. I know most children are not born on their actual due date (less than five percent according to an article written by Catherine Pearson on Huffington Post (Pearson, 2014)), but April 7th still is an important date to our family. After reading a lot of comments from grieving parents who have experienced stillbirth up-close and personal on an online social media forum, I realized that certain milestones and dates can be tough emotionally to face each year. The due date, their actual birthdate, and the day that you are given the unfortunate news your child has passed away, are all days that are imprinted on your brain (and heart) once you lose a child (or children).

Although many parents describe these milestones as being difficult, I wanted to take my lemons and make lemonade out of them by flipping a sour day into a joyous occasion. I didn't want to be sad or depressed on my son's due date every year, so I came up with an idea to celebrate his life through acts of giving. I chose giving, so I could use my platform as a grieving parent to acknowledge my son's existence all while helping someone else.

I coined the hashtag #DoGood4DJ as my way of celebrating my son's life. I asked all my family, friends, and social media followers to perform a random act of kindness on behalf of my son's legacy. I didn't necessarily want people to spend money, but I did want people to think of someone else, other than themselves for a day. The response to the first #DoGood4DJ was overwhelming. So many loved ones and friends participated in my simple request, I was beaming with pride knowing that my son's legacy was off to a great start. Many people expressed to me how helping someone else truly made their day. It surely made mine. I performed two random acts of kindness in honor of my angel DJ on his due date. I gave a random customer in Subway a $10 gift card to pay for her lunch. I didn't talk with her, I just walked in and paid for her lunch and walked out. The point of performing a random act of kindness is not to get recognition; it is to do something kind for someone else and ask them in return to pay it forward. I also took my nephews to the movies that day to see Zootopia. At the movie theater, I paid for a patron's snacks at the concession stand.

My acts of kindness weren't any huge feats but performing them made me feel good. It also made me feel like I was making DJ proud. I was using his tragic story to bring good to the lives of others. These kind gestures will never bring my son back but knowing that we could bring a smile to someone else's face even on a day that brings about a massive amount of sadness, what ifs, uncertainty, and much more, make it all worth it. All in all, I think I had over thirty people participate during my #DoGood4DJ campaign. The overwhelming feedback made my heart smile. So much so that I decided I would make it an annual event to honor my munchkin on his intended due date. My husband and I also decided that every year on January 18, we would celebrate our son's life in some capacity. Whether we have a cupcake and light a candle or release balloons, we will not let DJ's life fade into the background. We will acknowledge his time on this Earth and give him his proper recognition. We also discussed that when the time was right we would share DJ with his future siblings. We would let them know they had an older brother that was born an angel so that they can feel as close to him as we do. DJ's memory will not go in vain. He will be a celebrated fixture in our lives now until forever.

*Flyer I created for the #DoGood4DJ Campaign.*
*I used DJ's real footprints for the flyer and got them printed.*

*Ways to Remember Your Angel*

There isn't just one way to celebrate your child's life. There are so many things you can do to honor the legacy of your fallen angel. If you are at a loss or simply don't know where to start, here is a list of possible ideas you can use to jumpstart your creativity and recognize and remember your baby's legacy on your baby's birthday, due date, or any other significant date that reminds you of your baby.

1. Balloon Release
2. Butterfly Release
3. Memorial Service
4. Candlelight Vigil
5. Write a song in honor of your baby
6. Paint a picture that represents your baby
7. Write a book about your baby and your experience
8. Journal, then reread your journal entries on your baby's special day
9. Write a letter to your baby every year on their birthday and let them know how much you miss them and how you envision their life would be if they were still in your presence
10. Plant a tree in your baby's honor
11. Plant a garden in your baby's honor
12. Spread your child's ashes in a memorable location then go back and visit that location every year
13. Start a blog chronicling your experience of losing your child
14. Create or buy jewelry with your baby's initials that you can wear to remind you of them

15. Take a family trip in your baby's honor
16. Write a post about your baby on your different social media platforms on your baby's special day
17. Create graphics that remind you of your child
18. Take care of a plant in honor of your child
19. Display images of your baby wherever you feel comfortable
20. Make a memorial box and bring it out on these special days to bond with your angel baby
21. Start a foundation in your child's name to promote their legacy and help others
22. Create a support group where you can get other grieving parents together to comfort and support one another
23. Create a memorial walk or 5K in your child's honor
24. Give to a specific charity of your choice in your child's name
25. Create a scholarship or scholarship foundation in your child's name and honor
26. Name a star after your baby
27. Honor your baby's legacy on special holidays i.e. put up a stocking for your sleeping angel during Christmas or have a special basket set aside for your angel baby on Easter
28. Get a tattoo that represents your child i.e. footprints, angel wings, butterflies, feathers, name and birthdate, fingerprints, childbirth loss ribbon, etc.
29. Sponsor a child on holidays in your baby's honor
30. Take fresh flowers to the cemetery where your baby is buried

31. Make a special dinner and celebrate your child's life with your spouse, family, and close friends
32. Create a website that includes pictures of your baby, music that reminds you of your baby, journal entries, and a guest book for grieving parents to sign their names and their sleeping angel's names too
33. Create a playlist of songs that remind you of your baby and your pregnancy journey and listen to it whenever your baby crosses your mind
34. Look through your baby's picture or mementos on special occasions
35. Create a shadow box or space in your room to honor your child's legacy
36. Get a t shirt made with your child's name and wear it on their birthday or due date
37. Take family pictures and have a photographer Photoshop an image of your child or a shadow of a child representing your baby into the photo
38. Ask your friends and family to snap a picture whenever they see your baby's name i.e. on street signs, on a book cover, on a building etc.
39. Create a fundraiser to raise money for research towards pregnancy and infant loss
40. Say a silent prayer at the time your baby was born every day or just on your baby's birthday
41. Write a poem reflecting your baby's life
42. Make a physical or digital collage in your baby's honor
43. Etch your baby's name on a stone and place it somewhere safe
44. Purchase a wind chime, every time you hear it think of your baby's life

45. Engrave your baby's name on something and display it in your home
46. Wear jewelry that contains a keepsake of your baby i.e. a lock or hair or some of your baby's ashes
47. Have a diaper drive for an expectant mother who cannot afford them in your baby's honor
48. Make care packages for expectant mothers in shelters in your baby's honor
49. Celebrate Pregnancy and Infant Loss Remembrance Day on October 15, light a candle at 7 p.m. (and keep it lit for an hour) to honor your child
50. Release sky lanterns at the time your baby was born
51. Take memorial pictures at the cemetery where your baby was buried or with the urn
52. Make a scrapbook with your baby's keepsakes
53. Take a photo of something in nature that reminds you of your angel i.e. butterflies, rainbows, lights, dragonflies etc.
54. Purchase and name a crater on the moon in your child's name
55. Participate in a March of Dimes walk and walk in your baby's honor
56. Get involved with your local hospital's bereavement support group
57. Start a grieving parent's ministry at your church where you support other grieving parents by calling or sending a card or gift on significant days of loss etc.
58. Create a charm bracelet or necklace with specific charms that remind you of your angel, purchase a new charm each year

59. Order a Molly Bear
60. Have a custom portrait of your baby drawn or painted in their honor
61. Donate memory boxes to your local hospital
62. Order a Certificate of Life
63. Speak your child's name to anyone that will listen
64. Collect things that remind you of them
65. Send a note in a helium balloon to your child
66. Order a customized candle
67. Create a Shutterfly or Chatbooks album with all the important photos of your child and precious pregnancy memories (i.e. monthly bump photos, gender reveal pictures, baby shower and nursery pictures etc.)
68. Decorate your baby's gravesite
69. Make something special in honor of your baby i.e. jewelry, a painting, outfit etc.
70. Wear colors you associated with your baby i.e. the color scheme you were going to paint the nursery etc. on your baby's birthday or due date
71. Purchase the initials of your child using phone cases, wallets, keychains, laptop covers etc.
72. Create a craft with your baby in mind
73. Display your baby's name somewhere special
74. Get a custom Christmas ornament made with their name on it and hang it up during the holidays
75. Collect angel figurines or anything that reminds you of your baby
76. Add your child's name to your Christmas or Holiday cards (this is a personal preference)
77. Go to the beach and write their name in the sand and take a picture
78. Purchase your baby's birth stone

79. Bake a cake and sing happy birthday to your child on their birthday

80. Do a family photoshoot on your baby's birthday wearing something that reminds you of your munchkin

These are just a few suggestions on ways to celebrate your child's life during the holidays or special days that your heart remembers. You can do something on a grand scale or something a little subtler. Whatever fits into your family's aesthetic...do just that. I hope whatever you do, it is a helpful time of celebration, remembrance, and joy of all the good times and memories you have with your baby as well as a time of true reflection.

*After a visit to the beach this summer my husband
and I decided to leave a little message for DJ in the sand!*

*I'm always repping DJ no matter where I go!*
*I left his name on the sands of Destin Beach in Destin, FL.*

# Chapter 14

## Self-Care

*"For all who have entered into God's rest*
*have rested from their labors,*
*just as God did after creating the world."*
— **Hebrews 4:10** *New Living Translation*

Losing your child can be very mentally, emotionally, spiritually, and physically draining on you and your family. It is imperative that you practice self-care, so that you can take care of yourself during your time of grieving and loss. At the beginning, many people will be there to comfort you, assist you, and offer a helping hand along with their condolences. When your initial support system begins to fade (something that will happen inevitably as they expect you to get back to "normal") and you're left to pick up the shattered pieces alone, it is best to have practices in place to help you cope the best way you can. It is easy to spiral out of control when you lose someone so close to you, especially your child. That is why it is important to have parameters in place to help you begin to readjust to life without your little one present.

### Mental

There are so many things that will swirl through your mind on your grief journey. Some things may be things you may not want to even admit out loud. During your time of grieving and trying to figure out your new normal, your mind will be filled with various trains of thought. It is crucial that you try to quiet your inner voice and center yourself, so you can begin to think clearly and rationally. Ways you can practice self-care mentally is through meditation, through seeking outside professional help from a spiritual advisor, or a therapist. You can also read books that will assist you mentally to help guide you through grief as well.

### Spiritual

As a follower of Christ, I relied heavily on my relationship with God, along with my fellowship with my church family, as a way to cope with my loss. While you may not be attached to an organized religion, there are still some things you can do spiritually to help you expand your self-care routine. One of the many things I did and continued doing, was starting my morning out with a time of devotion and prayer. The quiet time I set aside with God allowed me to wake up and align my mind with His message to keep me sustained throughout the day. I used the devotionals to glean nuggets of wisdom on how to handle my loss in a productive way. Then I used my prayer time to communicate with God what I'd learned through my devotional time, to update Him on my personal feelings at that moment, and to ask for strength and guidance throughout the day to help me be strong in the face of adversity. I also used my prayer time to pray for all the other mothers, fathers, and families who had been directly affected by the loss of a child.

I often exercise faith as it offers hope even through my darkest situation. Faith is the substance of things hoped for, the evidence of things not seen. In other words, faith is believing that something will happen wholeheartedly before it happens, even if you don't know how it will come to pass. I used this faith to assure myself that life would get better soon, even if I didn't feel that way in that very moment. I also used my faith to know that pregnancy was not a death sentence and that I would have other children someday no matter how I had to get to that resolution. While I could never replace DJ, the fact that I could have children someday was a comforting factor. Faith is that blind hope that can carry you out of despair when you have nothing left to hang on to. I recommend you trying it out if you never have. What's the worst thing that can happen?

### *Emotional*

Emotional self-care is extremely important. You must know off the bat that you will have some good days and some not so good days during your time of grieving and thereafter. It is important to allow yourself the emotional release you need to go on throughout your day. One way I practice self-care emotionally, is by allowing myself time to express whatever emotion that arises. If I am sad, I give myself permission to experience sadness (listening to music that matches my mood, journaling about my sad feelings, crying, etc.). If I am upset, I allow myself the space to be upset. I usually do this by writing out my feelings, so I don't take it out on an innocent bystander. Another way to release anger in a productive way, is through physical activity (i.e. boxing, smashing plates/inexpensive china, kickboxing, dancing, going and shooting at a gun range, running etc.). Anger is a practical emotion that you experience during your grief process. How you use it and confront it makes all the difference.

Another emotional self-care tip, is to allow yourself to experience joy and happiness. Just because you experienced a tragic loss doesn't mean you are no longer entitled to participate in things that bring you happiness or exciting times in your life while you grieve. Allow yourself time to celebrate even in your grief. Manufacture experiences that make you happy. Treat yourself to ice cream. Take yourself to a movie or on a dinner date. Ask your spouse to accompany you on a trip out of town. Change up your scenery. Do something that makes you smile/laugh whatever that may be.

Part of self-care is releasing the emotions that are within you (as long as it is done without harm to you or anyone else). If you are emotional to the extent you feel that you cannot handle it, please do not hesitate to seek assistance. You don't have to carry this heavy load alone.

### *Physical*

After experiencing seven months of pregnancy, even if it was cut short, you notice the extreme changes your body undergoes to accommodate your growing passenger. For me, right after delivering my sleeping angel, I noticed a bevy of stretch marks on the side of my stomach, I noticed a protruding belly that once held a growing baby, and I realized that my frame expanded significantly (it was an uphill battle finding clothing that fit my growing body) I gained at least twenty pounds over the twenty-eight-week span of carrying my son. To practice self-care physically, it is best to try to take care of your recovering body. Give it the proper fuel by drinking lots of water, eating good stuff like fruits and vegetables, lean meats, and much more. And don't forget to find ways to squeeze in exercise, whether it's parking far away and walking further to get to the door, choosing the stairs instead of the elevator, or more formal forms of exercise like running, weight lifting, swimming, yoga, Zumba or any other activity that gets you up and moving. Another good tool to have in your physical self-care arsenal is scheduling massages regularly. I've never known anyone to turn down a massage. Massages have physical benefits for the body, but they also can help relax you and take your mind off your loss at least briefly.

All in all, it is an important step in grief management to incorporate acts of self-care. You owe it to yourself to be kind to yourself. You are worth the extra time physically, mentally, emotionally, and spiritually to set aside time out for yourself where you can focus solely on yourself and what you need to carry on daily. Don't let people guilt trip you in feeling that you cannot take a moment for yourself (even if you have additional children or a spouse). There are times when you just need a moment to yourself. Don't be afraid to take it! Remember, you can't effectively help others if you are running on empty.

# Chapter 15

## Insensitive Responses

*"There is one who speaks rashly*
*like the thrusts of a sword,*
*but the tongue of the wise brings healing." –*
***Proverbs 12:18** New American Standard Bible*

When you lose your child, you may notice that you will be bombarded with a sea of love, kindness, and encouragement. But mixed into the massive outpouring of support, you may encounter those who spew insensitive responses in reaction to your loss. You may even be shocked that some of these irresponsible responses will come from the people closest to you. It is best to prepare your reaction so, if or when these scenarios occur, you can be mentally prepared to handle them. There are many reactions that come along with loss. For people who are complete strangers or don't know that you lost your baby, they may come up to you and ask, "do you have any children?" or "why haven't you started a family, you're getting older?" or "how is the baby doing?" Any of these sentiments can or may drive you off a ledge if you're not prepared to face them head on. It is best in these situations, when you are dealing with insensitive remarks, to have a prepared answer at your disposal. You must decide how you will respond to those who may get you a little hot under the collar. Here are a few scenarios and possible responses to help you navigate through the turbulent waters of insensitivity.

### *"Do you have any children?"*

You should make up your mind early on how you will respond when you get asked this question. I personally say that I don't have any children when being asked by strangers because I don't want to go into detail about losing my son with a stranger. If it is someone whom I feel comfortable sharing, I will say that my son is in heaven and passed away at twenty-eight weeks. It depends on the comfort level I have with the person who asks the question. When I have more children in the future, I will probably say I have [insert the number of children] earthly children and one angel in heaven. But truly, it is a personal decision as to how you will combat being bombarded with this question. I must warn you, if you do say that your child has died, it can make the conversation uncomfortable very quickly. People usually feel squeamish when you bring up a baby that has passed away. But if that is what you decide you want your answer to be, that is totally ok. Say it with pride and confidence, even if it makes the other person uncomfortable. You have every right to speak about all your children if you so choose.

### *"Why haven't you started a family yet? Your [biological] clock is ticking."*

When people don't know you've suffered loss via stillbirth or any other type of pregnancy loss, they may ask you why you haven't started a family yet. It may rub you the wrong way because people don't know how hard you may be trying to conceive. When people see you with a baby bump, they may not understand the path you took to get to conception. They don't know if it took you a few weeks after ditching your birth control to become pregnant or if it took many years after constantly trying to experience the miracle of life. This is precisely why I hate when people ask, "when are you going to start a family," or "when are you going to get pregnant, because it is such a personal journey, filled with twists and turns. It is understandable if you are a bit annoyed when someone asks you this question. It may be good to just say *"when the time is right we will begin our family."* Or you can be honest and candid with people who probe so deeply and say we've tried to start our family, but we lost our babies on multiple occasions. I'm sure that will shut them up rather quickly.

### *"How is your baby doing?"*

For people who may not know you lost your baby, you may be asked how the baby is doing. I was hit with this question a couple times when going to the dentist or somewhere where they only see you once or twice out the year. I had to explain that I lost my baby at twenty-eight weeks during my pregnancy. When I give this explanation, it usually is followed with a host of "sorrys" or regret followed by an awkward tension that fills the air.

It can get uncomfortable, but you can and will get through it.

### *"When is your due date?"*

Again, for someone who doesn't know you lost your baby, they may ask when your due date is. Right after losing DJ, I was asked this question because I still appeared to be pregnant (even though I just delivered my sleeping angel). I again would let others know that my original due date was April 7; however, I lost my son on January 18 at twenty-eight weeks.

### *"Why don't you get over it already it's been [insert amount of time]?"*

After a loss, people usually are very sympathetic to you losing someone you truly love. But as time goes on they expect you and your feelings of loss to be dried up like water in a desert. This question may seem a bit insensitive to someone grieving, but it may seem like a logical question for someone who constantly sees you in a state of grief (at least in their eyes). It may be a good idea to let people know that just because time has passed from the moment you lost your fallen angel, it doesn't make it any easier to deal or cope with the pain of loss. It is wise to let people know who ask "why don't you get over it already" that you lost a child and will probably never "get over" the fact that you lost them. Your expression of grief may transform into something more "palatable" for others to accept but the longing of loss will always be present (even if you don't show it outwardly anymore). Don't ever let anyone rush you through your grieving process. Take the time you need to sort through all your emotions no matter if that takes weeks, months, or even years.

### *"It was all in God's will."*

While I am a professed Christian, the saying "it was all in God's will" is one of the phrases I heard that really burned my gears. This true but cliché phrase (usually muttered by those faith walkers who want something deep/profound to say) is more of an insult than a comfort while you're grieving the loss of your child. I know that God knows all and that He has a personalized plan for my life, but to say that my baby dying is in God's will is not a comfort at all. If you want to say something comforting to someone who has lost a baby because of a stillbirth, leave this statement off your list of encouraging things to say. While it may make the other person feel better to have something to say, sometimes, saying nothing at all and just being there is a better option than a sentiment that God wanted your baby dead for your own good.

### *"There must've been something wrong with the baby since it died."*

Again, this is another statement people make in trying to comfort you that comes off as a backhanded compliment. They try to imply that maybe you dodged a bullet by having the baby die early because something may have been wrong with them during the developmental phases of gestation. If you hear this statement uttered in your direction, you may simply respond by saying, "no matter what was wrong, with my baby, I would have still loved to meet him/her."

### *"When are you going to try again?"*

People don't think about the trauma that comes along with losing a child. But they really don't understand the backlash that trying for another baby has after losing a child. While having another baby seems like a logical step in "getting over" the baby you lost, we all know that that line of thinking is simply not true. Each baby and pregnancy come with its own process, experience, and emotions. If you are asked, "when are you going to try to have another baby after a loss," simply reply *"when my spouse/partner and I are ready."*

### *"Why are you being so dramatic, people lose people all the time?"*

Although death is a very natural part of life, it seems like a backward occurrence for a child to die before a parent. I wouldn't put a hierarchy of grief on any loss whether it is a parent, sibling, family member, close friend, church member, pet etc. but I can say that there are very different feelings and challenges that come along with losing a child, especially during pregnancy. Loss is inevitable in life, but you are valid for having a tough time dealing with the loss of your child. There is no shame in grieving your loss. If a person cannot see that losing a child is a devastating event, you may want to reconsider having them in your space while you are grieving or having them apart of your life at all.

***"Don't worry you can try again" or "At least you can have another baby."***

This is another response that seems harmless when first muttered, but it truly is an insensitive response. It may be true, you can probably try again (although you are not guaranteed to get pregnant again) or have another baby at some later date, but it doesn't erase the fact that you lost a child. **One baby does not replace another.** Even if you have another baby or a rainbow baby subsequently after losing a child during stillbirth, you still can never replace the child you lost, no matter how many children you have after the fact.

***"At least your baby wasn't forty-weeks-old when it died" or "At least you lost your baby during the first trimester. Imagine if you would've lost your baby at the end."***

No matter when you lost your child, whether in the early stages of your first trimester, midway through your pregnancy, right at forty weeks, or after your baby was born healthy with a steady heartbeat, the pain of loss sucks and hurts just the same. It may be easy to compare your timeline of loss with someone else, but the pain remains the same. At the end of the day, whether your baby was lost during miscarriage, stillbirth, a neonatal death, or infant loss, you still lost a part of you, no matter if your baby was in the form of a tiny bean on an ultrasound screen, in the form of a tiny fetus, a small one pound baby you could hold in your arms, or a fully developed baby who had gone through all forty weeks of its gestational process. No matter how the cookie crumbles, you lost a part of you, and that hurts regardless of your placement in the grief process. Some people may not truly understand that and may value or devalue where you were in your pregnancy journey when you lost your baby. Just understand that no matter how much value, or the lack thereof, that others place on your baby's life, it doesn't undermine that you were that baby's parent and they dwelled inside of you. You are allowed to express your grief freely no matter how far along you were along in your pregnancy.

### *"You're trying too hard."*

Although some people may wait awhile trying to start having children again, others may jump at the chance as soon as the doctor clears them to start trying again for another baby after a loss. Sometimes after trying and trying, a couple can experience a drought where they cannot get pregnant for a long period of time, or they may get pregnant but experience multiple miscarriages or stillbirths after their initial loss which can prompt someone to tell them they are trying too hard to have another baby. Being on the outside looking in, it may seem that you're trying to force something that is not meant to be, but for a person dealing with the emptiness of losing a baby, having another baby may be one of the only ways to mend their broken, grieving heart. I understand if it may be strange for people who have never experienced loss to say *"you're trying too hard"* but for those who have experienced the loss of a child or baby, it makes logical sense that you would want to fill the void when you're childless or have lost a child. Don't feel bad if you are trying to grow your family after a loss. Just make sure you are doing it for the right reasons. As long as you are happy, that is truly all that matters. Like I mentioned before, one child cannot replace another, but the joy felt with having another child can ease the pain of losing your own flesh and blood.

### *"You should just stop trying [after multiple miscarriages]. Maybe you should just try adoption instead."*

Some people may see you have suffered over and over from the pain of multiple losses and may try to throw out the suggestion that you should try to adopt. While adoption is a viable option to having additional children, it is not the answer for everyone. If you have suffered multiple losses, be sure to talk with your healthcare professionals to see if you can find out why you continuously suffer the same fate when trying to conceive children. If they say you are healthy enough to conceive, then by all means, do what makes you and your spouse comfortable. If you feel like you need to go down a different path i.e. In Vitro Fertilization, using a surrogate mother, or maybe even adoption, that is a decision only you and your partner can make. Don't allow people's perception of what you're going through deter you from doing what makes you happy when it comes to starting or growing your family unit.

### *"Everything happens for a reason."*

While everything does happen for a reason this may not be as comforting of a statement as people think. People don't realize the sting of losing a child unless they have lost one themselves. If you are hit with the "everything happens for a reason" line just reply, *"but I'm not sure why my baby had to lose his/her life in the process*." It may open more dialogue, but you must make people realize that just because they say something, in hopes it will comfort you (or to make themselves feel better or like they've done their part in sending their condolences), does not mean that their statement is comforting or acceptable in the moment.

### *"It was just a bunch of cells."*

The stage you are in when you lose your baby may change the response you get. In early pregnancy stages, people may not yet think of your baby as a baby. They may just think of your baby as "*a bunch of cells*," or "*a tiny fetus*." But as soon as you find out you are pregnant that is when you consider the life growing inside of you *your* baby, no matter how early on or late you are into your pregnancy. Just let it be known that you were the parent to the life you carried inside of you, no matter how many days, weeks, or months you got to spend with them.

### *"Maybe it was for the best."*

Again, here is another statement that people use when trying to comfort a grieving mother or father that isn't at all helpful. "*How can losing my baby be for the best?*" It's just one of those statements that people use to feel like they've said something comforting, but in all actuality, it is probably a statement they can keep to themselves. If you are hit with the "*maybe it was for the best line*" you can counter with "*maybe not, we'll never know*."

*"You should be grateful for the baby/children you already have" or "I hate to say it, but you have been blessed with [insert number] beautiful healthy kids, maybe you didn't need anymore" or "Maybe you have enough children already."*

My husband and I lost our first baby, but some people who deal with stillbirth experience this unfortunate mishap with subsequent children. Whether the baby you lost was your second, third, fourth, fifth, or twentieth it doesn't make a difference. The fact that you lost a child still hurts, no matter if you have more children or not. I didn't even have additional children at the time of my loss and it was very difficult to cope. So, I can only imagine what it feels like to try to go on as a mother and father with other children depending on you, all while trying to cope with your own grief and the grief that only a sibling can feel after the loss. Although I'm sure you are grateful for the other children in your care, it still doesn't bring back the one you lost. There is no shame in feeling bad for the child you lost while equally appreciating the children you do have! They are not mutually exclusive feelings. If someone tells you "you should be grateful for the children you have," ask them, "which one of their children can they live without" to put into perspective the toll/magnitude of losing a child.

*"Don't let this make you sad."*

I must admit, I don't think it is healthy to stay in a state of sadness all the time; however, I don't think you can get through a loss of a child without the emotion of sadness present at some point. Losing a child is devastating! There is no other way around it. Your child is not an "it" or a situation that can be handled. Your child was a human being growing inside of your womb. You were responsible for this life. It makes total sense that you would grieve for your loss of what could've, should've, and would've been. Like I've mentioned before, emotions are neither good nor bad they just are. But for those emotions like anger, bitterness, sadness, jealously, envy etc., you don't want them to stay around forever. But experiencing these feelings are very valid and normal to the grieving process.

### *"Better now than later."*

There is never a great time to lose a child. There isn't a time when you are planning for a child and suddenly that baby is taken from you, when it makes it easier on you as a grieving parent. To have the statement, better now than later, spewed toward you, is inconsiderate. Some may think because of your age (they may think you are too young), or because you are not married (they may think you should not have a baby without being married), or because of your life's circumstances (they may not think you are in the position to care for a child at the point you are in life) that may be a reason you lost your baby. None of those reasons will make you feel better when it comes to the thought of losing your child.

### *"Just try not to think about it."*

Again, trying to be forced not to think about your deceased baby is simply insane. You were planning to add someone to your family, a whole other human into your life. You can't just forget the fact that you had a baby growing inside you just because it makes other people feel awkward. Take as long as you need to sort out the grief, pain, and sorrow you feel that is associated with the loss of your little one. No one can tell you when your grieving time is up. Only you can decide that for yourself.

### *"You should get over your loss" or "You'll get over it."*

When you don't have to experience the loss of a child (or anybody for that matter), it is easy to say you need to just pick yourself up and get over it. But those who have stood on the front lines of grief, and know the true pain and agony of loss, and try to get their life back on track, know far too well that "getting over" your loss is a hard feat. While some may appear to get along better than others, loss is an individual bid each person has to go through. No one can give you a time limit on when they think you should be over the loss of your baby. Don't ever let anyone pressure you into feeling bad about grieving for a life you dreamed about. You get over your loss when you're ready, not when someone else, who is not dealing with the situation, says so.

### *"At least you don't have to worry about looking after a child with a disability."*

Sometimes children with disabilities or birth defects die during pregnancy. While having a birth defect or disability may increase the challenges for the child or parents it does not take away the fact that this baby was yours. No matter what you would've had to face as a parent, it still hurts just the same that you had to lose your child. Don't let anybody ever make you feel like just because your fallen angel had challenges, they didn't deserve to live, just like any other baby.

### *"Well at least you know you can get pregnant."*

Infertility issues are a real struggle that countless women face. While it is nice to get pregnant once, we all know from first-hand experience, it doesn't mean the subsequent attempts at conceiving will succeed. Knowing you can have children is half the battle, but that still does not negate the fact that the point of getting pregnant is to produce a healthy, bouncing bundle of joy after a forty-week period. If you simply get pregnant without the reward of the baby, what good does that do?

### *"You killed [y]our baby."*

Sometimes when you experience stillbirth, it is simply unexplainable. There is no rhyme or reason why your healthy baby just simply stops breathing or stopped having a heartbeat. In some instances, the cause of death can be figured out, while others are just freak accidents that cannot be explained. Sometimes your spouse, other family members and friends and in some instances, even yourself, may blame you for the loss of your baby, as you are the vessel or vehicle used to bring the baby into the world. Quite naturally, it may seem easy to heap blame onto yourself for having your body turn on your baby but resist the urge to blame yourself. Most of the time when you lose a baby during pregnancy there is really nothing you can do to change the outcome. Don't beat yourself up or allow anyone else to do so for that matter.

### *"Maybe it means that you are not ready to have children yet."*

This statement stings just as much as all the others. Losing a child does not mean that you were not ready. Most of the time it is some random fluke that occurs. It has nothing to do with your ability to be a parent. There is no reason you should be blamed for your loss, especially when doctors can't even find the cause of death.

### *"Try harder next time."*

Sometimes when you lose your baby during pregnancy, there are no viable signs to point to the cause of death. When you hear someone say try harder next time, that can be a slap in the face. To imply that you didn't try hard to have or save your baby is simply ludicrous. Try to block out ignorant comments like these when you encounter them.

### *"It probably happened because you're so young and not married"* or *"Maybe this wouldn't have happened if you were married."*

Some people truly believe the only way to start a family is after dating then getting married. If you have a baby before marriage, you may be judged by some who feel you are doing things out of order. No matter when you have a baby or your marital status, losing a baby hurts just the same. Don't let anyone guilt you into feeling that you were not worthy of having a baby just because you don't have a ring on your finger.

**"You wear your loss like a badge... you are way to open about it."**

Some people may be uncomfortable with you sharing your thoughts about your loss so openly. While openly talking about death may be uncomfortable for most, if talking about your baby helps in your healing, by all means do so. I would suggest you find people who will allow you to be candid and honest with how you feel. The people you share your grief story with may not be family members. You may have to look elsewhere to get the help and listening ear you need i.e. therapy, a counselor, a support group, a friend who has experienced something similar etc.

**"I'm pregnant! Why aren't you happy for me?"**

If you find yourself surrounded by someone close to you who was pregnant at the same time you were before you lost your baby, or they just found out they were expecting after you lost your baby, they may expect you to be overly excited for them. Although you may be excited for them, it may be hard to deal with seeing them pregnant since you lost your own baby. It is best to be upfront and honest with your friend or loved one about your emotional state and how you feel about their baby. Honesty and open communication can help you avoid many unnecessary and awkward conversations. You can simply let your family member or friend know that you are excited for them on their journey but that you are still mourning the loss of your baby.

While you may be unable to be there for them emotionally, you still are praying they have a safe, healthy baby. You may have to let them know that you have to distance yourself from them for a while until you feel comfortable being around their baby bump, the planning for important milestones i.e. baby shower, maternity shoot, announcements, newborn pictures, shopping for the nursery etc. Be sure to let them know upfront your boundaries so that you don't cause an unnecessary rift between someone you truly care about.

These responses are just some of the many insensitive remarks you may hear after losing your baby. I collected these scenarios from a group of moms who lost babies during various stages of pregnancy. Try to remember that most people say these things to try to be of comfort. If they really bother you, do not be afraid to speak up and tell people how their insensitive comments make you feel. You are the one that has to deal with the loss of your baby from the trenches. If statements like these continue to occur after you have already expressed your disdain for them, it may be time to distance yourself from these people or simply cut them off all together. Use your judgement to determine whether their statements are coming from a place of malice or just simple ignorance. As always, it is up to you to decipher what you will and will not deal with. Most of the time, if you let people know that their insensitive comments offend you, they will apologize and retract the statements. Just be honest and, nine times out of ten, things will work themselves out.

# *Chapter* 16

## Lessons I've Learned From Loss

> *"...Weeping may last through the night*
> *but joy comes with the morning."*
> – **Psalm 30:5 (Part b)** *New Living Translation*

There are many life lessons I was forced to learn from grief that I will carry with me forever. There are so many things we overlook, exposed by grief and loss. Here are some life lessons I picked up along the way after losing my son DJ to stillbirth.

### 1. *Life is short*

One thing I learned with losing DJ, is life is short. We typically hear this saying when people pass away, but it rang true when I stepped into my doctor's office with such anticipation and left broken-hearted. In an instant, my life went from being peaches and cream to being flipped and turned upside down. One ultrasound on a

Friday afternoon changed me forever. Since we know life is but a vapor passing through the air, we should do a better job living in each moment.

## 2.  *Cherish each moment (you don't know when it could be your last)*

Point number one leads me to my second point. Life is short; therefore, we should cherish each moment we are given. We never know when our last breath will be taken, so we should live life to the fullest today. Even in the most mundane moments, we still have something to cherish. I recently saw a Dove chocolate candy commercial that basically said live your life like you only have one day to live. If you were only given one last day to live, what people, places, or things would you align your agenda to do for the last time? This is how we should cherish the life and time we are given. Life and time are two things you cannot get back once they are gone. So, we might as well enjoy them while we are here, even if bad things happen like you losing your child due to stillbirth.

## 3.  *Be grateful*

While losing your child is nothing to celebrate, you can take a glass half-empty approach and turn it into a glass half-full moment. Although I was truly rocked to my core with the loss of DJ, he taught me to be grateful for the times I did get to spend with him. He lived inside me for twenty-eight weeks. In the grand scheme of things, that doesn't really seem that long.

However, through my grieving process I've learned to be grateful for the time I did have with him.

I got to spend a day with DJ after he was born. Although he was not breathing, was unable to open his eyes, or even make a sound his tiny presence filled me with a calm and peace like I've never experienced before. I was so grateful for the private time my husband and I got to share with him. It is something that will never be forgotten.

Even when you are going through your suffering, if you can find one thing per day to be grateful for, you will be surprised how your mood can change. Gratefulness has a way of shifting your perspective, even in your darkest hour.

### 4.  Communicate with those you love (often)

When I lost DJ, it made me realize you should be in constant communication with those you love. A short text that says, "Hi, I'm thinking of you," may do the trick in changing your mood. In my darkest hours of grief, it was nice to receive a random card, text message, phone call, or short email just letting me know that people were praying for me and thinking of Derrek and I during our lowest moment. It made me realize you never truly realize what people are going through daily and how your kindness through communication can brighten their day.

You don't have to make it a long drawn out thing. Just try to reach out to one person you haven't spoken to in a while. With social media these days, this shouldn't be a hard task. But for a more sentimental touch, use an old fashion stamp and letter and write a person a quick note just simply letting them know what they mean to you. I am positive they will be grateful for your kind gesture.

### 5. *Faith conquers fear*

There were always things I was scared to conquer, predating the loss of DJ, for fear of failing or appearing to be a failure. But after dealing with loss up-close and personal and facing fear head on, it made me realize, some things are simply not in our control, therefore, we might as well operate in faith and chase after those things we truly want out of life. Faith is simply believing something to be, although we may not see how it will come to pass. When we begin to see self-doubt creep in to try and block our faith-filled view, it is imperative that we quiet the outside noise and distractions and redirect our focus toward God. He will truly guide us and illuminate our paths if we continue to exercise our faith to take the next step.

### 6. *Trust in God wholeheartedly*

It may be hard to do this step at first, especially when you hear those dreaded words: "we can no longer find a heartbeat." You may get angry at God or turn your back on Him completely which are totally logical reactions to such a gut-wrenching experience. But I would say, don't stay angry or turn your back too long, because when the calls from friends and family begin to cease, and you are left alone to deal with your grief, there is one person who will never leave your side and that is God. God will be there for you when you have no one to turn to (not even your spouse or your parents). He will see you through. He has the masterplan for your life and He knows the greatness He has in store for you. You must buy into His plan for you.

7.  *Empathy*

Empathy is defined as the ability to understand and share the feelings of others. After joining the club of parents who lost children, I am now able to empathize more with parents who struggle to get to the forty-week finish line of pregnancy with a healthy baby that is born alive. I am even able to empathize more with parents who have premature babies that are fighting for their lives, or parents who have children with disabilities. At the end of the day, as a parent, you simply want what is best for your child. Being pregnant, what you truly want is for your baby to have a safe, warm, conducive environment to grow healthy and strong so that when the time is right you can assist (whether vaginally or through a caesarian section) their entrance into the world without a hitch.

I not only learned to empathize with families who have lost children, loss has also made me more in tune with those who struggle from every day mishaps and struggles. Everyone is going through something at some point or another in their life. It is easy to get lost in your own little bubble and want to compare and weigh the toll of your struggles to your neighbor. But we all have moments in life where challenges arise, and the burdens are too tough to bear alone. That is when empathy goes a long way!

8. *Sympathy*

The definition of sympathy is the feelings of pity or sorrow for someone's misfortune. Sympathy allows us to connect with humans on a basic level. It allows you to look at a situation and say, although I am not going through the same exact thing as you, I can find pity or sorrow in the fact that you are hurting, suffering, going through a challenge, etc. It is important as grieving parents to operate in a sense of sympathy and empathy even in our own grief. It truly helps identify with people on a deeper level when you can recognize that everyone goes through something that is life altering whether that is the loss of a child, spouse, parent, job, house, etc. As Dionne Warwick stated in her popular song, "what the world needs now, is love, sweet love." We all are here on Earth trying to navigate our own life's journey. The best thing we can do to make that journey a bit easier, even with the non-avoidable ups and downs, is love. Self-love and love offered to all mankind can change our world for the better!

### 9.  *Love on your spouse/significant other*

The loss of a child can take a toll on various relationships in your life, especially that of your spouse or significant other. It is very important to give your spouse wiggle room to grieve for the loss of your child in their own individualistic way. It is also important to routinely ask your spouse/partner if there is anything you can do to help them through their grieving process. It is imperative to open the lines of communication with your spouse/partner, so they know exactly how you are feeling about the loss of your child and you can understand where they are coming from on the matter.

Don't be afraid to compliment your spouse during your time of grief. Losing your child can be such an isolating experience. To have the heightened care and attentiveness of your spouse/significant other is helpful, especially on those days when you feel down. A small/simple compliment can go a long way. For instance, if your wife looks particularly nice, let her know. Or if your husband has been doing a phenomenal job around the house making sure the chores are completed, thank him and compliment him for the help.

Find time to create laughter even in your grief. It may be a tough thing to do at first, but trust me, laughter makes the soul happier. It also makes your burdens seem a little lighter, even if that is just something that is psychological.

Have fun with your spouse/partner. Don't let grief stop you from enjoying things you both like to do (separately and together). If you both like to go hiking, or skating, or do cross-fit, make plans to do those things. Check out a new restaurant in your area, movie hop, or have a romantic picnic in the park. Carve out some time for the two of you to enjoy each other's company and create a system of reliability, so you know you both have a shoulder to lean on.

Do something spontaneous for one another. A few weeks after I loss DJ, my thirtieth birthday rolled around. I knew for sure I wanted to get out of town for my birthday for a change of scenery. My husband surprised me with a birthday trip. He told me the amount of days we would be gone and what types of clothing items to pack. Everything else was out of my control (the location of the trip, lodging, activities, dinner plans etc.). By doing something spontaneous, I was appreciative that he thought enough of me to plan an entire trip from start to finish. It was a very kind gesture. One that will never be forgotten.

Trust each other. During the process of grief, you will discover that so many things will begin to look uncertain. But one thing that remains the same, is the love you have for your spouse/partner. Don't be afraid to be vulnerable with your spouse/partner. They are experiencing the same tragic life event you are. Find consolation and comfort in that. Elevate your trust in one another to higher levels even amid your pain and sorrow.

Say thank you to your spouse/partner when they do something kind for you, no matter how minute or grand the gesture may be. When someone thanks you for doing something, you feel appreciated. It is important to feel appreciated especially during your time of sorrow. Don't be stingy dishing out thank you's.

Lastly, don't be afraid to apologize if you accidently hurt your spouse's/partner's feelings by being dismissive about how they are feeling or through their grieving process. As I've mentioned time and time again in this book, we all grieve differently. There is no set way to experience grief. We must be open to accepting how our spouses/partners choose to grieve and give them time to heal the best way they know how, even if it differs greatly from our own grief process.

All in all, draw closer to your spouse/partner. They are your biggest ally through this entire ordeal because they have a front-row seat to the experience of tragedy and loss. Don't shut them out, no matter how bad you want to. Keep the lines of communication open, offer compliments, be each other's support system, laugh, do fun things together, be spontaneous, trust one another, say thank you, and apologize when you do something to offend the other. If you do these ten things with your spouse/partner routinely, I promise you your relationship will blossom to something beyond your belief.

## 10. Transparency

I mentioned before that talking about my son was a huge part of my grieving process. By talking about him, it helped me validate his existence and the pinnacle role I played as his mother. It also helped me to sort through the entire ordeal and glean the amazing parts of my pregnancy. I never sought out to talk about my baby publicly for the sake of likes or sympathy. I truly did it selfishly to help me feel better. In the process of my candidness, I realized that I was helping to set others free. I by no means take the credit. I believe God is continually using my tragedy and loss to help others see there is light after the darkness. You can still have a healthy marriage, graduate with honors, sing praises to God, excel in life, have a positive mindset even after a tragedy such as mine (or yours).

I never set out to be a pillar of strength to others suffering loss or simply going through life's hardships, but that seemed to be the case the more I shared my story of loss, hurt, grief, gratefulness, peace etc. I truly just opened my heart and penned messages of loss and hope to my blog readers, followers on various social media platforms, or even to my friends in person and received an overwhelming outpouring of love and support from many who I never knew were even paying attention to my situation. You never know how what you're going through could help someone else. I would never have volunteered to be a spokesperson/mother of stillbirth, but in a weird way, I am grateful the Lord chose me to go through this ordeal. It has been life altering in more ways than I could have ever imagined. Just by simply being transparent and showing my good days along with pulling back the curtain on my bad ones, I've established a relatability and likeability like never before. I am forever grateful and humbled by this experience.

## 11. *True love*

I thought I would only get to experience true love once in my life and that was with my husband, who is simply an angel living here on earth. But I never knew how much I could love another being (outside of my husband) more than that of the love I have for my son. From the first time I saw his heart flicker on the ultrasound monitor, to the time I held his lifeless body in my arms, I grew an immense amount of love and awe for him like nothing else I have ever experienced. I'm sure all parents (those of children that are living and/or deceased) can attest to the joys children can bring. It is an indescribable feeling. Just admiring every crevice of my son's tiny body brought me to tears. I could just sense the amazing human he was even though he was only a few hours old. While I didn't get a chance to experience his personality or spirit, I could tell from the energy he brought into the room that he was a very special kid. No matter how many children come after him, he will always be my first-born munchkin. I will love him for eternity. He has taught me so much! I can never fully repay him for the life lessons he taught me, even at twenty-eight weeks old. He was truly a miracle in my life that will never be forgotten.

## *12. Sacrifice*

When you hear the story of how God sacrificed Jesus to eradicate the sins of the world, you don't understand the magnitude of the sacrifice he offered. Mary and Joseph (Jesus' earthly parents) had thirty-three years to marvel in their son's amazing life, yet they still had to deal with the fact that their son was sent to earth to be the sacrificial lamb. He was sent merely to take upon the sins of the world for people who were his enemies, so that we may inherit eternal life later down the line. Talk about a selfless act of love, kindness, and sacrifice. I grew up in church, so I heard countless stories of Jesus repeatedly. How he died on the cross, sacrificing his own life, so we as sinners could potentially inherit the kingdom of God and start with a new blemish-free record.

Putting our loss into perspective made me realize just how hard it must have been for God to devise a plan knowing His only son would be killed, essentially to take the rightful place of sinners who had disobeyed Him. I cannot imagine volunteering the life of my son, DJ, to help save the world but that is what Jesus did for us. I have a newfound appreciation for the sacrifice He offered for those like me who were yet sinners, but He still took my place. I lost DJ, but it taught me that my loss would not be in vain. DJ's life was sacrificed in order for me to gain humility, empathy, sympathy, peace, deeper faith, a stronger relationship with God, my husband, my family, friends and more. All in all, at the time of sacrificing something it usually does not feel good. But when you reap the benefits of your sacrifice, it will all be worth it in the end. Am I suggesting that it was best for our babies to have died so we can learn first-hand the lesson of sacrifice? **Absolutely not**! I am simply stating that, removed from your grief, you can see how sacrifice in life is a necessary evil used to ultimately help us grow.

### 13. *Understanding*

I gained a newfound understanding of what it means to be a parent. It also made me particularly grateful to my own parents and how they raised me, as well as thankful for my mother-in-law and father-in-law for how they raised my husband. Just giving DJ back was simply put one of the hardest things I've had to do in my life. Watching his small body rolled out of my hospital room for the last time was a gut-wrenching sight. At that moment, I understood how some parents sacrifice their well-being for the betterment of their children. If asked could I switch places with my son so that he could live, I would've traded places in a heartbeat. But God saw fit for something else. So, I am left here reshaping my understanding of life and what it means to truly be a parent. While I don't have a physical baby to show for it, the day we found out we were expecting DJ, we became parents. I tip my hats to all parents, those who are parents to earthly children and those who have the privilege of being parents to angels, because parenting is not an easy feat.

### *14. Stopping and smelling the roses*

It's important, even as you travel along your grief journey, to stop and smell the roses. It's cliché but its sentiments still ring true. If you don't make it a point to enjoy the things that make you happy in life, to have a grateful heart, mind, body, and soul you can get overworked with the mundane of life. But it truly is a matter of perspective and looking beyond the surface to find the beauty in all things. No matter what those things may be. It is important that you live in the moment. Don't take things for granted and simply take in all that God has blessed you with.

### *15. Confidence*

My baby taught me to be confident in who God made me to be. Right now, I am the mom of an angel. I am confident in this title because God has showed me that I have blessings in store that He hasn't even released yet. I am truly confident in the woman I am becoming, the wife I am growing into, the mom I so desperately want to be, etc. Confidence is radiant (not to be confused with cockiness or arrogance). It allows you to take pride in the person God created you to be when He knit you in your mother's womb. You can be confident in who you are becoming because you are the only one like you on this earth. Even with billions of people around the globe, there is still not one person who is exactly like you. We may share similarities in skin color, race, ethnicity, personality, interests etc. but no two people are exactly alike which breeds a confidence in just simply being uniquely who God destined you to be!

## 16. *I Shouldn't Fear Death*

As I mentioned previously, I never really had someone super close to me die before. Death always seemed like such a scary, daunting experience. But to be honest when I was faced with death head on, I realized it's not as scary as it once seemed. I looked at my son face to face as he laid lifeless in my arms and felt at peace. It sounds kind of weird to say holding my dead child made me happy, but in that instance, all was right with the world. A quote also brought me comfort in my time of mourning "*...And to think when he opened his little eyes, the first thing he saw was the face of Jesus*" – *source unknown*. It is comforting to know that if my baby cannot be in the arms of my husband and I, then the next best place for him to be is in Heaven with His ultimate creator, Jesus. It makes my grief pill a little easier to swallow.

## 17. *What True Peace Looks Like!*

It is amazing to experience true peace. I mean peace so deep that you can smile when your whole life is falling apart. After planning to invite a baby into our home for seven months, my husband and I were awakened with a nightmare of losing him all in a matter of twenty minutes. If I didn't have God or ask Him for peace, I know for sure I would have been dead, depressed, or angry with the entire world. If those are feelings you've experienced through grief or you are currently experiencing, this is not to put you down or place blame on you. Know there is life after the depression, the anger, the sadness etc. You can truly experience peace if you align yourself with God. He can bring a feeling of peace over you that may shock you. I was amazed at how well I took on grief. There were definitely days I would weep on end, or snap for no reason, but I always reverted to that home base of peace. It made a world of a difference. If you have been searching for that inner peace and are trying to experience a calm like none other, just say this simple prayer: ***"God please grant me inner peace in my time of grief. Allow me to experience joy even in my pain. Guard my heart from hate, sadness, and depression and fill it with peace, love, and gratefulness. In Jesus' name, I pray. Amen!"***

### 18. *How a Consistent Prayer Life Can Be a Major Asset*

Whenever I felt so low that I couldn't talk to anyone, I would either pull out my journal and jot down my feelings or pray. Or I would do both. It is amazing how being candidly honest with God can set you free. On the days, I was feeling drained with tear stained pillows, I would cry out to God for strength. On the days, I was filled with gratitude, I would thank God for allowing me to parent and give birth to such an incredible human being. On those days, I would feel blah, I would simply tell God exactly how I was feeling. It felt good to be able to release whatever feelings I was feeling inside. It always drew up a song to my memory bank I learned when I was a little girl. "*I cast all my cares upon you. I lay all my burdens down at your feet. And anytime I don't know what to do. I will cast all my cares upon you.*" When I cast my cares and burdens at the feet of God through prayer, He always had a way of lightening my load and offering me a stillness like no other. I dare you to give prayer a try. It simply is a way we communicate with God. I am transparent and real when I speak with God. I let Him know my emotional state and ask Him for guidance (even though He already knows). Prayer is an amazing outlet to have while you are going through your grieving process.

### 19. *How to Follow Your Goals and Dreams While You Have the Chance*

When you lose someone so suddenly you realize life is not promised. You could be here today and gone tomorrow. So why not go after the things you truly want in life. You never know when your time here on Earth will be cut short. It is best to live your life to the fullest. Those dreams, goals, and plans that you have for yourself, your partner, your marriage, your job, your life, your family dynamic, why not try to pursue them with reckless abandon. That way if you do pursue your dreams and life ended today, you would know you gave it your all! I am a firm believer in speaking things into the atmosphere and letting the universe know what it is I have a desire for. I do this by creating vision boards and constantly writing out my goals, dreams, and plans. When you write things down and make them plain, say and declare things out loud, and you visually create reminders of what your dreams are, you give your subconscious a reminder of what you want out of life. When those things start to come into play you begin to get overjoyed because you know you worked hard to achieve those things, causing you to dream even bigger and bolder dreams!

### 20. Boldness: Be Authentically You

After losing your child, you recognize life is short, so there is no need to pretend you are something you are not. I learned with my loss that I am a flawed individual who has some amazing qualities. While losing my baby was tough on me emotionally (and most days I felt very weak), I was told that through my sharing of what I was going through and how I was feeling, I was strong. That took me by surprise because in my weakest moments, I realized how strong I truly was! It helped me to walk in a newfound confidence and accept myself for who I truly am; flaws and all!

### 21. Don't be ashamed or afraid to share the tough parts of life, it humanizes you when you authentically share.

Being authentic is something that is truly missing from society today. With social media, people handpick and even manufacture stories and pictures showing you the best parts of their lives. You've seen that one Instagram account or Facebook post where you simply envy or admire the life someone else is living. You know the one where they are happily married, with 2.5 kids, a beautiful home with a white picket fence, a dog, amazing car, dream job, money in the bank, trendy clothes, travel around the world, partying it up in mansions and on yachts, or they're beautiful with the aid of a banging contoured face and hairstyle to make Queen Bey jealous, they have the perfect body, a great group of friends, tons of followers and the list goes on and on and on. But the truth is life is not always so perfectly wrapped in a bow. While pictures say a thousand words, they don't always tell the entire story. You may see me smiling, and in that moment, I am happy. But you don't see me when all the lights are off, and I'm awake during the wee hours of the morning, bawling my eyes out.

I said all that to say, on the days when I shared the toughest parts of my life during my grief journey, those were the days I received the kindest words. People are tired of seeing the perfect lives that we manufacture for social media. They find comfort in knowing that even though I am happily married, highly educated, well-traveled, and liked by many, that I too go through struggles, and the toughest one yet was losing my son. I showcased this part of my life, not for sympathy or even for likes, but because I saw through my sharing I was helping others overcome tough times that they too faced. While our struggles differed, the feelings of hopelessness, sadness, redemption, forgiveness, faith, new found hope, joy, and even gratitude are universal themes that many people can connect with. Don't be afraid to share your story (no matter how un-pretty it may appear). You never know who you may be helping in the process by simply sharing your unadulterated story. Someone is always watching you, so be mindful of the story you tell.

## 22. *Don't Be Afraid to Speak Up for What You Want and Need*

I've always been a people pleaser for as long as I can remember. It's part of my nature. I've always loved to help others, and sometimes at the detriment of sacrificing helping or speaking up for myself. In the act of losing DJ, I learned that I am the best advocate for myself. You can't worry about what people will think or what they will say about you. You must ask for what you want and speak your truth. Sometimes my mission to please others left me depleted, tired, and empty. Through this experience, I learned to say NO! It's okay if you don't feel up to something and you decline an invitation. I learned I had to take time out for me. I couldn't worry about how others were grieving about the loss of

DJ because I too was trying to sort through my own feelings. It's not a bad thing to be selfish sometimes. You can't be a help to others if you don't take care of yourself first. Don't be afraid to speak up for what you want and need during your time of loss. If you need space, vocalize that. If you'd rather be in the midst of company, invite the people who you want to spend time with over. If you think you need to talk to someone find a person you can confide in. If you'd rather not talk about your experience with others that is fine too. Just do what absolutely makes you happy, and don't apologize if it goes against your norm.

### 23. *Let It Go (don't harbor on negativity, hate, pettiness, shade, etc., instead dwell and walk in positivity, love, understanding, and offer a helping hand to those who need it most)*

When dealing with grief, it is quite easy to get in a headspace of negativity, hate, anger, pettiness and much more. Losing someone can make you much more cynical. It is my suggestion that while it is okay to experience these raw emotions, it is not okay to stay in a place where these emotions linger too long. Nobody wants to be around a sour puss. I understand that the experience you are going through is very traumatic and it can cause you to put on your "glass half empty" pessimistic lenses, but I dare you to try a different approach. Instead of going the classic "oh woe is me" route, try spending a day walking in positivity, love, and understanding, even if you have to fake it, until you make it. I guarantee, if you use your time in the spirit of gratitude, thanking God for the time you did get to spend with your sleeping angel (no matter how long or short), or if you are able to do something for someone else without expecting something in return, your life will be filled with blessings overflowing. Even if that simply means you can smile through the pain. Or still identify the beauty in the world after such a tragic loss.

### 24. Forgiveness (to self and others)

After losing a child, it's easy to place blame on everyone for what happened, including yourself. But you must understand that some things are simply not in our control and the best way to move past any situation is to offer forgiveness, so we can heal and grow. One thing my therapist suggested I do, was write down all the people I could place blame on, then make it a point to forgive them. One of the people whom I harbored the most angst toward was the ultrasound technician. The way she made me feel in my last ultrasound appointment where I ultimately found out my son had no heartbeat was very uneasy. I blamed her for the sadness of losing my son. But I realized I needed to forgive her because she was simply doing her job when an unfortunate situation occurred. I also realized in my forgiving, I needed to forgive myself. I blamed myself and my body for not being a safe-haven where my son could grow into a healthy, living, forty-week old baby. When I decided to forgive, I felt a freeing spirit take over me. Forgiveness is a necessary part of the grieving process. I suggest tackling forgiveness early in the process.

Like my therapist suggested, I recommend taking a quiet, designated time to write out all the people you knowingly or secretly hold a grudge against after the loss of your child. Then one by one write down why you have alleged angst against that person and the role they played in your child's death. After your list is complete it is time for the hardest part, FORGIVENESS. It is time to forgive those whom you deem responsible for what happened to your child. Once you do, you will feel a weight lifted off your shoulders. Remember, the best way to conquer this exercise is to be totally honest and open with yourself on who you harbor anger against so true healing and forgiveness can take place.

**25. *No Matter How Dark the Day May Get the Sun Will Come Out Tomorrow (Weeping may endure for a night, but joy will come in the morning)***

Tomorrow may not necessarily mean the day after the current day we are in. But just know as time passes on, your grief will become easier to tote around. One year into my grief journey, I can honestly say that the load of grief (while still there) has become a lot lighter to carry. I still miss my son EVERY DAY, but I can find more joy in the fact that he is in a better place, that he was the most handsome baby I've ever laid eyes on, that

I was blessed to have spent twenty-eight weeks of his life with him and much more. You will experience some tough days ahead, but hold tight, stay strong, and keep the faith and all will work out just fine. Just you wait and see!

# Chapter 17

## Conceiving Again & Rainbow Babies

*"⁵Trust in the Lord with all your heart and*
*do not lean on your own understanding.*
*⁶ In all your ways acknowledge Him,*
*and He will make your paths straight."*
*– **Proverbs 3:5-6** New American Standard Bible*

### *Accepting anxiety that arises when trying to conceive again*

Deciding that you are ready to try for another baby is different for every grieving couple. Some couples decide they want to try to get pregnant right away after losing a child because they cannot bear the hollowness going home empty-handed from the hospital. They decide they want to hold a baby in their arms sooner versus later and may have a one-track mind on getting pregnant again. Other couples may put off having a child for few months or a few years, to try and cope with the emotions and feelings losing a child drums up within. They may need time to heal and work through the tragedy of losing the baby they were growing inside, and how it affects the dynamic of their new family unit. Some families may ultimately decide that trying to conceive another baby is unbearable and simply not in the cards for them. If you no longer want to attempt to start or grow your family after loss, that is totally acceptable. As long as you and your partner are on the same page that is all that matters.

When we found out we were pregnant with DJ, my husband and I never had a game plan to get pregnant, we simply talked to my doctor about the possibility of pregnancy and one month later I was expecting. Although we weren't planning to get pregnant right away, we welcomed the idea of adding a new bundle of joy to our lives.

I would be lying if I said I was not anxious to get pregnant again, but there wasn't a strict timeline to become pregnant. After DJ's death, I mourned his loss daily for a solid three to four months, writing Facebook posts about him, journaling, and much more. I even went to counseling. It is there that I believe I started to fully come to terms with what truly happened to me and started to make strides in my healing. Only then could Derrek and I even discuss the possibility of trying again for another baby.

There were certain times throughout our trying that I thought I was pregnant. I bought at least six pregnancy tests that all came back negative, which surprisingly really shook me to my core. Once you set your mind on the fact that you want to conceive again after loss, you can become focused with the idea of having another baby. So much so that it can turn into an obsession. Every time I urinated on that stick and saw a negative or minus sign a chunk of my heart was ripped out and I became saddened. I would come back to a place where I would think...*why am I even doing this? I should have a healthy little baby boy in my arms right now, enjoying the newness of mommyhood and parenthood with my husband. Instead, all of that was snatched away and I had to start from square one.* If you let them, these types of sentiments can drive you insane. During my time of trying to conceive, I had to pray regularly to ask God to help focus my mind on the positives and not so much on the negatives.

It is best to keep in mind that when trying to conceive, a lot of emotions will probably bubble to the surface. You may feel like you shouldn't even have to start over again with the process of trying to conceive when you were already pregnant. You may feel like you need a baby ASAP to fill the void of losing a child, which can cause you to become super focused on having another baby. You may put off having children for years because your fear will not allow you to be set up for another possible let down of losing another child. You may hesitantly try to conceive again as you try to sort through your divided mind of wanting another baby but not wanting to go through the process again. You may even turn to an alternative of having kids like adoption, IVF, or choosing a surrogate mother to carry your child for you. No matter which headspace you are in at the time...extend yourself leniency! You've just suffered something that a select few truly understand. The magnitude of losing a child is monumental and long-lasting. It is not something you can just simply brush off and forget. It is something that stays with you. Allow yourself the proper time to begin healing (however long that may be for you and your partner) and trust that when the time is right you will be blessed to begin your journey of conceiving again.

### *Rainbow babies*

According to Kicks Count, the definition of a rainbow baby is "a baby that is born following a miscarriage, stillbirth, neonatal death, or infant loss (Kicks Count, 2014)." Rainbows by nature are beautiful, bright, colorful wonders that appear after a storm. In the Bible days, rainbows symbolized a covenant between God and His chosen people. Rainbows represented God's direct promise to His people. To boast a rainbow baby is to know the flip-side of the coin. **Loss!** Finding light in darkness or sunshine after rain is a huge step in the recovery process.

Becoming pregnant again, after losing your child, can be a daunting thing. The blissful, blind optimism of conceiving, waiting nine months, then delivering a healthy bundle of joy is no longer present. Families that have suffered the loss of a child know that at any moment, within a forty-week time span, the life of their growing child can be cut short. It's an unfortunate way to think but it is the reality of parents, siblings, grandparents, etc., who have lost their children during pregnancy across the globe.

When you lose your child, it is important to give yourself as much time as you need to help cope with the side effects that come along with the trauma of grief and pain accompanied by a loss. For some, trying to conceive quickly is the answer to filling the void in their empty hearts with the space of a new pregnancy or new baby. While one child can never replace another, the feeling of being pregnant again allows some women to feel like they can carry out the task of carrying a healthy baby for nine months and delivering that baby without the feeling of loss or hopelessness looming over them. For others, they may need to put some space in between the death of one child to conceive a new one.

While totally immersing myself into healing using the five stages of grief (see page 101, Chapter 7: Grief's Rollercoaster, for a refresher on the five stages of grief) as my reference point, I was able to experience a glimmer of hope in the midst of tragedy by conceiving my rainbow baby, Grayson Derrek Anderson, six months after losing our son DJ. We weren't necessarily planning to get pregnant again, but I happily welcomed the chance to get another crack at mommyhood a second time around.

After officially confirming my pregnancy with my doctor, I was filled with an overwhelming sense of appreciation and gratitude for creating a new bundle of joy. Although I was entrusted to carry a new life, I must be candid, the flipside of expecting a rainbow baby was daunting at first. Finding out you are pregnant again after loss, can usher in a whole new wave of emotions you don't initially account for, on top of those grief-filled emotions you already harbor for your angel baby. It was a tough transition in the beginning to get excited about the new life that was growing inside me because fear, worry, and anxiety took up major real-estate in my headspace.

Instead of blissfully daydreaming about what my baby would look like, what having another boy would mean to my husband and me, what type of nursery he would have, items to put on my registry, cute clothing that would make my son look adorable, or researching key first-year items, I began thinking: *"I've been down this road of expectancy before. It is familiar territory."* My mind continuously reminded me, in DJ's case, how we made it over the first trimester hump, halfway through the second trimester, and into the final stretch of pregnancy. But ultimately DJ being abruptly snatched away from us, was life altering. I could not fathom diligently putting in the work toward healing from grief, getting pregnant again for the second time around, making it pass the twenty-eight week mark or all the way to forty weeks and beyond only to have my rainbow baby succumb to the same fate of death's angel like his older brother DJ, because the pain would be unimaginable. So, I begged, hoped, and pleaded daily through prayer that this time around would be a different outcome.

After reading a book, that my mom recommended titled, *The 4:8 Principle* by Tommy Newberry, my entire mindset about my second pregnancy changed. One concept the author mentioned was that you cannot curate a mind of negative thoughts and expect to manifest a completely opposite outcome of positivity. Two dueling thoughts cannot coincide in your mind at the same time. One thought will have more clout than the other. Eventually you are going to have to choose which team of thinking you want to join. *Team Fear or Team Freedom?*

I realized after completing the 4:8 Principle that I was living in terror of losing my rainbow baby, but I wanted to hold a healthy living baby at the end of my forty-week journey. Those two thought patterns were total contradictions of one another. After reading that powerful book, I decided from that day on, I would only speak positivity and life into my pregnancy. I would choose anticipation, excitement and gratitude for the new life that was formed and shaped in my womb over being a slave to anxiety, fear, and worry. When I traded my fear for faith, and my being terrified for total trust in Christ, that was when I started to truly enjoy my pregnancy (back pains, feet swellings, sleepless nights and all) despite the rose-colored glasses of pregnancy bliss being removed.

I will caution you, trying to stay optimistic for nine straight months and not fully caving into fear, worry, or anxiety can be difficult if you allow it to be. You can be doing ok one day, excited about your little bundle of joy growing inside you, the next moment you can be reminded of your fallen angel, and without warning, your optimism and happiness can fade back into fear and anxiety if you choose to let it creep in. Being pregnant with a rainbow baby is like carrying a Great Dane while you are trying to balance on a high-wire tight rope, hundreds of feet above the ground. It requires extreme focus on the task at hand while trying to balance your emotions of happiness and sadness, excitement and terror, highs and lows and much more.

If I could give one piece of advice when going through a subsequent pregnancy after a loss…it would be just take it one day at a time. My first pregnancy with my son DJ, I got so far ahead of myself. I was planning trips in my head, working out the logistics of my parents and in-laws coming into town to help take care of the baby. I planned out his baby shower, nursery, newborn photoshoot, and outfits. I'm a blogger, so I was going to begin incorporating my son as a reoccurring visual contributor to my blog. What I learned through the loss is that you should cherish each moment, because nothing is promised or guaranteed, especially when it comes to pregnancy.

Another word of advice I would suggest, is figure out how you want to incorporate (if at all) your angel baby with your new bundle of joy. Will you tell your new baby about their sibling that passed away? Will you incorporate your sleeping angel in your announcements to announce the arrival of your new bouncing baby (i.e. DJ is going to be a big brother April 2017)? Whatever you choose is your prerogative. At the end of the day no two pregnancies are alike.

Once you announce you are with child again, many people will move their focus onto your new bundle of joy and rush to shower you with happiness and celebration, but we as parents in the exclusive club of loss know that while having a new baby is an absolute blessing we still want to honor the child(ren) we loss. We try to make sure the baby who suffered still has a place in our hearts, minds, and in the world. There is no replacing the baby we lost, but the rainbow baby is a great reminder that life continues. To have a rainbow baby is to have a heart in constant battle. Your heart will always mourn for the loss of your fallen angel you so tragically had to give back. But the flipside is that your heart also holds an unsurmountable amount of love and adoration for your new baby after such a tragic loss. It is truly the definition of a real-life balancing act.

I would also mention that even though you lost your child (in our case our first born) doesn't mean you cannot celebrate the life of your new baby. You don't have to walk around in black and gray mourning the loss of your child without acknowledging your new baby. It is not an insult to your angel baby to celebrate the new life growing inside of you. It may be tough to navigate through all the milestones of pregnancy a second time around, but it is not impossible. While I still think about DJ daily, I was in a parallel universe where my mind was also on Baby Anderson #2. Does it make me a bad mother not to acknowledge the two at once all the time? Of course not! It simply makes me human. I tried to find a happy medium with keeping DJ's name, life, and legacy alive while trying to prepare for the life that we would share with Baby Anderson #2. At times, being pregnant with your rainbow baby can feel like you're experiencing déjà vu or that you're walking in a dream that soon may become a nightmare. It's like you're waiting for the shoe to drop. That is why it is imperative to do what feels best to you when you deal with pregnancy after a loss.

When Derrek and I were pregnant with DJ, we waited thirteen weeks to spread the news to our immediate families because we wanted to get out of the "dangerous first trimester" before spreading the good news. The second time around Derrek and I decided to tell our parents and siblings that we were expecting right away so we could have a much-needed support system as we went through our journey again. We also decided we would not tell the world about our pregnancy until we felt the time was right, which was after week twenty in a Christmas card sent to very close family and friends. A few weeks later, after our small inner circle of family and friends were made aware of our tiny blessing, we made our announcement on social media when I could no longer disguise my ever rounding baby bump. There is no right or wrong answer here. We simply did what felt right to us. There is no manuscript that accompanies the loss of a baby. It is a personal journey that every parent must experience and write their own manual to as time progresses. Just remember, without the rain, there would be no rainbow.

To share our news about our second son, Grayson, we decided to do a photoshoot that announced we were expecting along with the sex of the baby. I kept Grayson's sex under wraps until we sent out Christmas cards with a photo collage of pictures we took from our photoshoot. The pictures turned out so amazing. When we shared them with our friends and family they were so excited to share in the joy of our amazing blessing that came in the form of a rainbow baby.

### *What happens if you no longer want children or want to conceive after experiencing loss?*

As I mentioned earlier in this chapter, there is no shame in not wanting to try again to have another baby. The stress of conceiving and officially expecting again can have a major effect on your family mentally, spiritually, financially, and emotionally, especially if you continue to experience the devastation of loss again and again. If you decide after your loss that children are no longer in the cards for you, just know that is a reasonable conclusion to consider. Just be honest with yourself and solid in your conviction. You can always fill the void/space where you initially wanted your child or additional children to go with pets, or a hobby like traveling. Please don't think if you don't have another baby after loss, your life cannot be complete, because that is completely false. The narrative of moving forward after loss is shaped by you (and your spouse/partner). If you want more children after loss, by all means go for it. But if you don't want more children, fill your life with something that brings meaning and purpose beyond the pitter patter of little feet filling your home.

*Photoshoot with B–O–Y balloons to share we were having a baby boy!*

*Daddy giving Baby Grayson kisses!*

*Showing off my noticeable baby bump!*

# Chapter 18

## Second Time Around – My Rainbow Baby Is Here, Now What?

*"I have set my rainbow in the clouds
and it will be the sign of the covenant
between me and the earth."*
— **Genesis 9:13** *New American Standard Bible*

Can I be honest with you? In the beginning of my pregnancy, I was afraid to get attached to the small seed growing inside me for the fear of losing him, but by the end of my third trimester, I could not wait for his arrival. You may not yet be at the stage where you are celebrating the arrival of your very own rainbow baby. You may still be in the early stages of grief (which is totally understandable – don't rush your grief process. Take as much time as you need to heal before moving forward with getting pregnant again). But, if you do get to that point of expectancy again, if that is something you desire, I suggest that you make the most of your pregnancy by doing some special things to help you celebrate new life after experiencing a loss. Here are some things I did to make the second time around a bit more special and memorable.

- Take frequent pictures of your baby bump – *it helps to chronicle just how big your tummy is getting.*

- Video record your ultrasounds – *I asked my husband to video record the ultrasounds when the sonographer showed us our little fetus moving around in my belly.*

- Record your baby's heart beat – *Because I was told that my first son no longer had a heartbeat, I cherished the sound of my rainbow baby's heart; so much so that I recorded it and saved it on my phone. I listened to it often on days when I felt my anxiety starting to creep in.*

- Document your pregnancy through video or audio updates using a mobile device, computer, or tablet or go old school and write in a special pregnancy journal about how you are feeling each day, by incorporating vivid bump growth pictures, or by scrapbooking etc. – *While I was pregnant, I would make video logs (vlogs) about how I was feeling [mentally] that particular day. I also gave updates about where I was in my pregnancy. It's an awesome keepsake to have video chronicling your journey with your rainbow baby.*

- Incorporate your angel baby into your rainbow baby's baby shower – *My shower planner knew*

*how important my angel baby DJ was and still is
to me, so she thought of subtle ways to
incorporate his legacy into my baby shower (you
can read more details on that in "My rainbow
themed baby shower" section below) for my
rainbow baby.*

- Sing, talk, pray, read, etc., to your baby in your
belly – *Communicate with your [rainbow] baby
while they are still in your belly. Create good
vibes and positive energy around them so they
know they are loved.*

- Talk to your rainbow baby about their angel
sibling (even while in your belly) – *Mention your
angel baby to your rainbow baby even while they
are in your belly, so they know the importance of
the role their deceased sibling plays.*

### *My rainbow themed baby shower*

Early on during my second pregnancy, I knew I
wanted to have a rainbow-themed baby shower. As
mentioned earlier, rainbows have various meanings for
different people, but to moms who have experienced loss,
rainbows are quite special. They represent new life.
Second chances. Survival. Blessings and much, much
more. So, when I stumbled across a rainbow themed
shower on a party-planning website, Oh Happy Day
(www.ohhappyday.com), I was blown away at how
amazing the set up looked. It captured the mood I wanted
to exhibit and inspired me to fully tell my stillbirth story
of love, loss, and triumph through an awesome prism.
After seeing the inspiration for the shower, I showed my

awesome friend Ashley W., and we began planning my shower. I gave her the basic vision of how I wanted the shower to look and run, then she executed it flawlessly with the aid of my mother, cousin, aunt, grandmother and mother-in-law. She made decorations and even made me a rainbow necklace that correlated with the theme (and matched my DIY pom-pom rainbow sandals).

The shower was held at a quaint event space. The aesthetic of the space was just what I envisioned: clean cut and minimalistic. We packed the room full of vibrant colors to help replicate the rainbow. I even challenged all my guests to wear one solid color from the rainbow in solidarity, to help celebrate the life of *both* my sons, Grayson, my rainbow baby, and my fallen angel DJ! Having my guests show up in various color combinations of the rainbow was probably one of the highlights of my shower. We took pictures at the end with all the guests separated into their respective R.O.Y.G.B.I.V *(red, orange, yellow, green, blue, indigo, and violet)* rainbow color groups, holding up the corresponding specially-handcrafted large scale building blocks that spelled out my son's name: **G-R-A-Y-S-O-N.**

Another amazing part about my shower was the attention to detail my party planner, Ashley executed. She created a table in the room that had a scrapbook on it along with an elephant and giraffe. We asked all the guests to write well wishes in the scrapbook for Grayson and special notes for DJ. When I got home and read the thoughtful sentiments from each of my guests I was almost moved to tears. The gesture was so kind and something I can keep forever. The elephant on the table had Grayson's initials (G.D.A) alongside the giraffe which had DJ's initials (D.J.A). The elephant signified the theme for Grayson's nursery while the giraffe represented the safari theme I was going to use for DJ's nursery theme before he was abruptly taken away from us. Having a moment to explain what a rainbow baby was, along with the amazing table honoring DJ and Grayson, was just awe-inspiring.

At the end of the shower, I gathered all the balloons that were used as decorations and my husband and I released them back up to our munchkin in heaven, while my close family and friends looked and cheered us on. We even videotaped the encounter so that we could have that special memory of dedication and thanks to our angel for years to come. It was the end to the perfect day. When the time is right, we can show our rainbow baby, Grayson just how much his older brother meant (and still means) to us.

*My rainbow delivery story*

After my baby shower, I literally had one week before I delivered my rainbow baby six weeks early!!!! My husband and I just bought paint and supplies to paint our son's nursery. Since his name is Grayson, I wanted to paint an accent wall gray. Friday evening, on March 3, 2017, around 8 p.m., my husband busted out the paint along with the various supplies we had purchased earlier that day and began painting the nursery. After a couple of hours of painting, we both showered and relaxed before going to bed around midnight. Being that I was about eight months pregnant, my large belly and I were sleeping on the couch at this point in my pregnancy because it was too inconvenient and uncomfortable to try to roll in and out of my high-sitting bed to use the restroom at night. During the wee hours of the morning, I had one of many of my routine potty breaks. After using the restroom, I came back and took my position on the couch when I felt a sudden gush of liquid.

I knew that I didn't urinate on myself, because I had just left the restroom, so my mind rushed to the next explanation. Earlier that very week in our pre-delivery childbirth class, our instructor discussed the stages of labor. She mentioned when your water breaks, you first will see your mucous plug release then you will feel a gush of liquid follow. There was no question. My water broke! After the initial shock of my water breaking, I rolled off the couch and calmly but with some urgency, walked into my bedroom to inform my husband that I believed my water broke. Since we weren't 100 percent sure, we decided to go to the hospital just in case it was not a drill. We quickly threw on the nearest clothes we could find, grabbed our cell phones and booked it to the hospital.

The ten-minute drive to the hospital went by in a flash. We were buzzed into the Women's Birthing Center at the hospital around 4 a.m., then escorted to a temporary waiting room. In that room, I explained to the nurses that I believed my water broke. They asked me to get into a robe and then they proceeded to check my cervix to see if my water had broken and if so, to check how far dilated my cervix was. Come to find out I was already dilated four centimeters when I arrived at the hospital, so they admitted me right away. By 5 a.m., I was in a delivery room getting hooked up to IV's and getting pricked and poked. **WE WERE HAVING OUR [RAINBOW] BABY!!!**

Once the initial shock wore off that we were about to have our baby *that day*, we called our parents and informed them that I was in labor, and it was only a matter of time before their grandson would make his entrance. The next few hours, I played the waiting game until around 10:30 a.m., when my contractions really started picking up. I knew early on, prior to coming to the hospital, I was going to opt for an epidural again. Once the contractions became a little too strong, I informed my nurse that I wanted the epidural. They prepped me and gave me the shot by 11 a.m. Once I received the epidural, and my lower half numbed, my nurse returned and checked my cervix. She felt my son's head crowning and told me it would only be a matter of time before my son entered the world. About a quarter to twelve, the doctor arrived, and it was show time. It was time to push.

I pushed for about fifteen to twenty minutes before I heard the screams of my handsome five pound, five-ounce, nineteen-inch long, premature baby boy. Grayson Derrek Anderson entered the world at 12:21 p.m. Saturday, March 4, 2017. When he made his debut, all was right with the world in that instant. All the pain of loss, all the tear-stained pillows, all the sorrows of wearing the badge of a stillbirth parent to an angel, vanished the moment I laid eyes on my son. I finally was able to breathe a sigh of relief after eight months of anxiety, doubt, fear, worry and excitement; so, I thought.

When Grayson was born, the nursing staff tended to him, while the doctor helped me safely deliver my placenta. After Grayson was all cleaned up, I planned to do skin-to-skin contact before my first official attempt at breastfeeding. I had envisioned this moment from the first day I found out I was pregnant, holding my baby boy against my chest, skin to skin, heartbeat to heartbeat connected in pure bliss. Just as I was about to bask in the glory of the birth of our son, one of the nurses calmly grabbed Grayson and said that he was laboring to breathe properly. They didn't want to scare me but wanted to monitor him for the next hour or so in the neonatal intensive care unit (NICU). So just like that, my rainbow baby was whisked away to the NICU. While I was relieved that Gray had made his entrance into the world, I was bummed that his arrival didn't quite go as I planned.

One thing I've come to understand from my loss of DJ to the birth of Grayson, is the fact that pregnancy is indeed unpredictable. While we have preconceived notions of what the perfect pregnancy and delivery looks like, it rarely seems to turn out how we imagine it. The biggest hurdle of a rainbow baby is just getting them here safely without any hiccups! Although I was blessed to hold my baby in my arms alive, it did not happen without its own set of challenges. After spending a week in the NICU (battling respiratory issues, jaundice, and much more) we were finally cleared to take our munchkin home! At last, I was able to release my inhibitions when I strapped Grayson into his car seat and we drove away from the hospital with a healthy, living, tiny, but mighty baby boy!

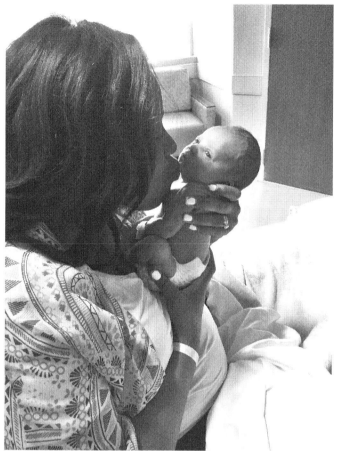

*Me marveling at my five-day-old rainbow baby, Grayson!*

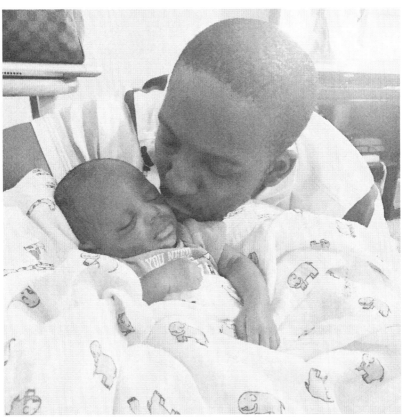

*Grayson getting kisses from Daddy!*

### *Blessings of having a rainbow baby*

While we've encountered crying fits, sleepless nights, dirty diapers, hundreds of spit ups, the challenges of breastfeeding and much more, we wouldn't have it any other way. Grayson has blessed our home like none other. From all the hurt we dealt with from our first son passing away, it felt like we were finally being rewarded after the storm, with our pot of gold at the end of our rainbow. We've made so many memories in the short period of time Grayson has been on this Earth. He has brought such joy into our lives. But we will never forget the sacrifice we had to make to get to this point.

If you are contemplating whether you can handle trying for your rainbow baby, I suggest you go for it. While your emotions may be all over the place with the fear of loss looming over you, don't let it paralyze you to the point of inaction. Trust me when I say, the risk is worth the reward! Once you gaze into the eyes of your precious rainbow baby, you will get to finally experience the joys of parenthood. No child can replace another, but a rainbow baby is an awesome constellation prize for going through the knock out, drag out, gut punch being a stillbirth [baby loss] survivor brings.

### *What happens if your rainbow baby never comes*

As grateful as I am for my rainbow baby, I understand, not everyone is guaranteed a fairytale ending, resulting in child birth. While I consider myself an optimist, seeing life's jar half -full, I recognize the harsh reality, rainbow babies after loss are not always in the cards for all baby loss/pregnancy loss families. And that is perfectly okay. Although Grayson has been an amazing addition to our family and an all-around blessing, I recognize not all baby loss survivors stories end like mine.

Some baby loss families must utilize alternative methods to get pregnant like rounds of In Vitro Fertilization (IVF), which can be very costly and does not offer a 100% guarantee of getting pregnant and having a baby. Some baby loss families get pregnant with the rainbow baby they prayed for, only to discover their baby will be born with a disease, birth defect, or incurable disorder, forcing them to yet again shift their paradigm to create a "new normal" of what parenthood looks like. Others may suffer loss after loss and decide adoption is the best route for starting or rounding out the family they've always dreamed of. Some baby loss families may try with no avail to get pregnant but may be forced into accepting their unplanned lot of childlessness.

While children are a huge blessing and parenthood is one of the greatest accomplishments and challenges in life, if you do, or do not ever get the opportunity to conceive again (after loss), I stopped by to tell you…You are whole! You are loved! Your life still has meaning and purpose with or without a physical baby in your arms! Most importantly, you are STILL a mother or father even if others cannot see or choose not to recognize your sleeping angels.

# Chapter 19

## Holding On, While Moving Forward

*"For I know the plans I have for you, "says the Lord.*
*"They are plans for good and not for disaster,*
*to give you a hope and a future."*
*– Jeremiah 29:11 New Living Translation*

The journey ahead is going to be tough, probably one of the toughest things you will have to endure in your entire life. There will be days when you don't feel like you can take another step, or even go on. You will feel like the world is crashing down on you and that your life is no longer your own. Your happiness and joy of being pregnant may turn into the very thing that crushes your soul after your loss. But be assured that just because you are down-trodden now and feel all hope is lost, does not mean you will stay in this position forever. I'm here to tell you from first-hand experience, that there is light at the end of the tunnel, there is love at the end of the tunnel, there is gratefulness at the end of the tunnel, and there is purpose at the end of the tunnel. You must keep pushing and moving forward to get to it. Don't let grief keep you locked down in a personal prison. Use your grief to emotionally release, to take inventory of where you are and where you want your life to go and continue to use your grief as fuel to take one step each day toward healing and a new-found purpose.

One thing is certain. Time does not stop, and life goes on. While I would do absolutely anything to have DJ back in my arms, I know that's not a possibility in this lifetime. But it doesn't take away my memories of him. It doesn't erase the time we spent together for twenty-eight weeks. It doesn't erase the love I have for him and will continue to feel for him for the rest of my life. Although it is hard to let go and say goodbye to the physical presence of your baby, you never have to let go of their memory and what they represent to you! That is the biggest lesson I've learned on this journey of grief. There is no correct way to do it. You simply do the best you can with what you have. It is best to surround yourself with a tribe of people who will encourage you to do what is best for you and who will allow you to grieve in any way you deem necessary to help you start life anew.

I truly hate we had to meet this way, in an exclusive club for parents who have suffered the unthinkable loss of a child, but I hope that throughout this book you have been able to find relief in knowing that your angel was not here in vain, that we will forever be connected through our tragedies, that triumph is always on the other side of tragedy, and that you can and will make it, no matter where you are currently, on your grief journey!

I pray a mighty blessing on you and your family! I pray that your good days will outnumber your bad ones. I pray that you will gain strength through your trials. I pray that you can come out victorious even after one of the worst things in your life has taken place. And most importantly, I pray that once you find your footing and climb your mountain peak of grief, you will look back, reach out, and pull someone up who may be struggling in their own personal grief journey. We are all a family now, bonded by our bad misfortune of losing beautiful angels. But the story does not have to end here. We can make it… and we WILL be victorious in the end. All because we are **STILL HERE**!!!

# References

Centers for Disease Control and Prevention. (2017, October 2). *Fact About Stillbirth*. Retrieved December 19, 2017, from Centers for Disease Control and Prevention: https://www.cdc.gov/ncbddd/stillbirth/facts.html

Harmon, K. (2011, December 13). *U.S. Stillbirths Still Prevalent, Often Unexplained*. Retrieved from Scientific American: https://www.scientificamerican.com/article/stillbirth-risk-factors/

Kicks Count. (2014, March 14). *What is a Rainbow Baby?* Retrieved from Kicks Count: http://www.kickscount.org.uk/rainbow-baby/

Oxford University Press. (n.d.). *Stillbirth*. Retrieved December 19, 2017, from Oxford Dictionaries: https://en.oxforddictionaries.com/definition/stillbirth

Pearson, C. (2014, September 22). *New Guidelines For Estimating Women's Due Dates Issued By OB-*

*GYN Group*. Retrieved from Huffington Post: https://www.huffingtonpost.com/2014/09/22/estimating-due-date_n_5862754.html

PhD, C. G. (2018, February 14). *The Five Stages of Grief*. Retrieved from Psycom: https://www.psycom.net/depression.central.grief.html

*Information About Stillbirth*

## THE STONE – COLD FACTS ABOUT STILLBIRTH

According to Oxford Living Dictionaries (Oxford University Press, n.d.) **Stillbirth** is *"The birth of an infant that has died in the womb (strictly, after having survived through at least the first 28 weeks of pregnancy, earlier instances being regarded as abortion or miscarriage)."* The Centers for Disease Control and Prevention (CDC https://www.cdc.gov/ncbddd/stillbirth/facts.html) describes stillbirth as *"The death or loss of a baby before or during delivery* (Centers for Disease Control and Prevention, 2017). *"*

## THE NOTEABLE DIFFERENCE BETWEEN A MISCARRIAGE AND STILLBIRTH

"Both miscarriage[s] and stillbirth[s] describe pregnancy loss, but they differ according to when the loss occurs according to the CDC (Centers for Disease Control and Prevention, 2017). In the United States, a miscarriage is usually defined as loss of a baby *before* the twentieth week of pregnancy, and a stillbirth is loss of a baby *after* twenty weeks of pregnancy (Centers for Disease Control and Prevention, 2017).

## CLASSIFICATIONS OF STILLBIRTHS

Stillbirth can be further classified as either *early, late, or term* according to the CDC (Centers for Disease Control and Prevention).

- An *early* stillbirth is a fetal death occurring between twenty and twenty-seven completed weeks of pregnancy.
- A *late* stillbirth occurs between twenty-eight and thirty-six completed pregnancy weeks.
- A *term* stillbirth occurs between thirty-seven or more completed pregnancy weeks.

## THE STATISTICS OF STILLBIRTH

How many babies are born stillborn each year you ask? "According to the 2015 National Center for Health Statistics report stillbirth effects about one percent of all pregnancies (Centers for Disease Control and Prevention, 2017). Each year about **24,000 babies** are born stillborn in the United States (Centers for Disease Control and Prevention, 2017)." "The number of stillbirths in the US each year is about equivalent to the number of babies that die during their first year of life, but unfortunately is ten times as many deaths as the number of deaths that occur from Sudden Infant Death Syndrome

(SIDS) (Centers for Disease Control and Prevention, 2017)."

## WHAT INCREASES THE RISK OF STILLBIRTH?

The causes of many stillbirths are unknown (Centers for Disease Control and Prevention, 2017). Therefore, families are often left grieving without answers to their questions. Stillbirth, is not [an actual] cause of death, but rather a term that means a baby's death during pregnancy (Centers for Disease Control and Prevention, 2017). Some women blame themselves, but rarely are these deaths caused by something a woman did or did not do [during her pregnancy] (Centers for Disease Control and Prevention, 2017). Known contributors to stillbirth generally fall into one of three categories:

- Problems with the baby (birth defects or genetic problems)
- Problems with the placenta or umbilical cord (this is where the mother and baby exchange oxygen and nutrients)
- Certain conditions in the mother (for example, uncontrolled diabetes, high blood pressure, or obesity)

Stillbirths with unknown causes are called *"unexplained stillbirths* (Centers for Disease Control and Prevention, 2017)." Having an unexplained stillbirth is more likely to occur the further along a woman is in her pregnancy (Centers for Disease Control and Prevention, 2017).

Although stillbirth occurs in families of all races, ethnicities, and income levels, and to women of all ages, some women are at higher risk for having a stillbirth. Some of the factors that increase the risk for a stillbirth include the mother (Centers for Disease Control and Prevention, 2017):

- Being of black race
- Being a teenager
- Being 35 years of age or older
- Being unmarried
- Being obese
- Smoking cigarettes during pregnancy
- Having certain medical conditions, such as high blood pressure or diabetes
- Having multiple pregnancies
- Having had a previous pregnancy loss

While the CDC works to learn more about who is experiencing stillbirths and why (by tracking how often stillbirths occur and researching causes and preventative measures of stillbirth), they still have a long way to go (Centers for Disease Control and Prevention, 2017). This book is an account of my personal story of loss through stillbirth. While I specifically talk about the loss of my son through stillbirth at twenty-eight weeks in this memoir, stillbirth is not the only form of baby/child loss during or after. Other forms of baby loss include but are not limited to: *miscarriage, neonatal death, or infant loss* (Centers for Disease Control and Prevention, 2017).

In this book, you will see me recount my experiences as a stillbirth mother (and survivor). However, there are overlapping themes that **all** baby/child loss parents can relate to. Don't think that just because you or your loved one experienced baby loss in a different way other than stillbirth that you cannot glean nuggets of hope and encouragement from this book. This book is here to be a companion during your grief journey after losing a child through any form of baby loss.

It is my prayer, as the author of this book and a fellow baby loss survivor, that you will find comfort and condolence, and unlock answers to questions you may have buried deep within during your grief journey, while reading this book. Use this memoir to self-reflect, reminisce on the good times, but most importantly, use this book as a tool to jumpstart your recovery and find healing to the devastating blow that is baby loss.

## Books

Here are a few books I read through my grief journey that pointed me towards the path of healing and restoration.

- Still by Stephanie Paige Cole
- The 4:8 Principle by Tommy Newman
- Instinct by T.D. Jakes
- The Secret by Rhonda Byrne

## Digital Support Groups

After birthing DJ, I knew I needed some support, whether it be in person or in a safe, online forum. Here are some digital closed Facebook groups I've found helpful through my stillbirth grief journey.

- The Angel Mom Alliance by Jolie Bloom – Miscarriage and Infant Loss Support
- Stillbirth Babies – Forever in Our Hearts
- The Grayson Project Birthday Wishes (Stillbirth & Infant Loss)
- Forever Angel Babies Support Group
- Still Birthday Support Circle
- Pregnancy and Infant Loss Awareness
- First Candle Stillbirth Support

*Hashtags and People to Follow on IG Who Represent Baby Loss Well*

These are hashtags I used and individuals I followed on Instagram that encouraged me through my stillbirth journey.

- #stillbirthsurvivor
- #stillbirth
- #stillbirthawareness
- #stillbornawareness
- #stillbornstillloved
- #pregnancyandinfantloss
- #rainbowbaby
- #rainbowmama
- @jheanelladams
- @joliebloom
- @ameilakyoga
- @ericammcafee
- @kennedysangelgowns
- @mommy.bewell


*Music*

Here are some songs I used to create a playlist when I miss my little munchkin, DJ. While I sometimes use these songs as an emotional release, they always make me think of my angel!

- *A Thousand Years by Christina Perri*
- *Always Be My Baby by Mariah Carey*
- *Angel by Lalah Hathaway*
- *Angel of Mine by Monica*

- *Can't Help Falling in Love by Haley Reinhart*
- *Dreaming of You by Selena*
- *How Do I Live by LeAnn Rimes*
- *I Could Fall in Love by Selena*
- *I Hope You Dance by Lee Ann Womack*
- *I Miss You by Aaron Hall*
- *I Will Always Love You by Whitney Houston*
- *I Will Trust You by James Fortune*
- *I'll Be Missing You by Diddy Ft. Faith and 112*
- *Landslide by Dixie Chicks*
- *Missing You by Brandy, Tamia, Gladys Knight, & Chaka Khan*
- *Missing You by Case*
- *My Heart Will Go On by Celine Dion*
- *Need You Now by Lady Antebellum*
- *Officially Missing You by Tamia*
- *One Sweet Day by Mariah Carey and Boyz II Men*
- *Please Don't Go by Immature*
- *See You Again by Wiz Khalifa Ft. Charlie Puth*
- *Small Bump by Ed Sheeran*
- *What Hurts the Most by Rascal Flatts*
- *Why I Love You by Major*
- *You Should Be Here by Kehlani*

*Websites*

Here are a few websites that helped me throughout my stillbirth grief journey.

- Jolie Bloom: http://www.joliebloom.com
- Centers for Disease Control and Prevention: https://www.cdc.gov/ncbddd/stillbirth/index.html
- March of Dimes: https://www.marchofdimes.org/complications/loss-and-grief.aspx
- Erica M Mcafee: https://www.ericammcafee.com

*Baby Loss Holidays*

Here are a few baby loss holidays you may want to add to your calendar to acknowledge and celebrate your sweet angels.

- **May 6:** International Bereaved Mother's Day
- **August 22:** National Rainbow Baby Day
- **August 26:** International Bereaved Father's Day
- **September:** Neonatal Intensive Care Unit (NICU) Awareness Month
- **September 16 – September 22:** World Childless Week
- **October:** Pregnancy & Infant Loss Awareness Month
- **October 15:** Pregnancy & Infant Loss Awareness Day

# Acknowledgements

I first want to acknowledge God. Thank you for using me as an instrument to offer healing to millions of grieving parents and families around the globe. Thank you for using me as a vessel to spread the good, the bad, and the ugly truths, along with the hope after losing a child via stillbirth.

Next, I want to thank my amazing, supportive husband Derrek Anderson. You are my biggest cheerleader and my #1 supporter. You always encourage me to go after my dreams and keep me accountable when I begin to slack. You are the yin to my yang, the lemon to my lemonade, the honey to my bees and the love of my life. I could NOT have made it through this tragic experience without you by my side. Thank you for drying my tears, holding me when I needed to be held, sitting with me in the silence, propping me up when I felt weak, and letting me share my most intimate frustrations, sadness, small victories, and memories about being a stillbirth survivor. I am forever grateful for your selflessness and couldn't ask for a better helpmate. I love you, bae!!!

Thank you to my parents who each played a vital role in me moving forward in this never-ending grief journey. Thank you to my mom for coming down to sit with us in the hospital when DJ was born. Thank you for being our personal secretary for a couple days, our personal chef when we came home from the hospital, and a listening ear when I wanted to talk about DJ and my experience as a mom with a heavenly prize! Your motherly love was much needed in the toughest time of my life, and I appreciate it more than you ever know. I also want to thank my dad for being the spiritual representative on our behalf. Thank you for interceding for our well-being during this time. Thank you for taking the initiative to spread the news to family, so I didn't have to recount the tragic scenario over and over again and thank you for planning the memorial for DJ during my graduation. It was the perfect ending to a great day. It meant a lot that you thought enough about DJ, Derrek, and I to want to plan such a sentimental moment to solidify DJ's legacy in our family. I will never forget that day and that kind gesture. I love you and mom greatly.

I want to also thank my brothers, Phillip (Loren) II and Dion; sisters-in-law, Grace and Kisha; nieces and nephews for thinking of me, calling me, texting me, caring for me, and praying for me during my time of grief. I've always looked up to you all and to know that you guys had my back during my lowest point, really meant a lot. I will never forget your generosity.

Thank you to the most awesome mother and father-in-law, Valarie and Darwyn Anderson, who both called, prayed, visited, and checked on Derrek and me regularly. I was truly blessed when it came to hitting the in-law jackpot. I wouldn't trade either of you for the world. Thank you from the bottom of my heart.

I want to thank all my extended family: my brothers-in-law (Derryn and Derrius), grandparents, aunts, uncles, cousins, and close friends (you all know who you are…there are so many of you to name) for being the most amazing support system. You guys sent food, cards, money, plants, flowers, fruit baskets, books, well-wishes, prayers, love, support, encouragement and much more to Derrek and me when we needed it the most. I am blessed beyond measure to know that I have such an awesome village of people to lean on when I am at my worst. I thank you all and want you to know I love you more than you'll ever know.

I want to also acknowledge my therapist, Dr. Holly Brown. Thank you for being an outside point of view, a listening ear, a spring board to launch ideas, and a sound voice of reason to help me navigate the waters of grief, hope, recovery, anguish, discovery, confusion, emotions, and much more when it got tempestuous. I am so grateful to have met you. I feel our meeting was a divine step on my grief journey.

I also want to thank my amazing head nurse Ginger Burress, the amazing Houston Medical Women's Center nursing staff, my remarkable doctor, Dr. Susan Thomas at Houston Medical Center and the McCullough Funeral Home in Warner Robins, GA for making my hospital stay stress-free, memorable, and comfortable even during one of the roughest times in my life. I will NEVER forget the lengths you all took to make DJ's legacy memorable (the photos, the one-of-a-kind keepsakes, the blankets, outfits, free cremation etc.).

Lastly, I want to thank each of you for reading this book. It has been a labor of love. I would not have been able to write it without you all in mind. While I am sad you had to pick this book up because you or someone close to you has experienced the loss of a baby through stillbirth (neonatal death, infant loss, or miscarriage), I pray that this book has helped you (or your loved one) on the road to recovery and discovering your "new normal." I pray sunshine, love, happiness, and ultimate blessings over your families. Just know God says He will never leave us nor forsake us (even in our darkest moments), and remember He is always there and so am I. If you need to chat, have any questions, want to say hello, or just want to get something off your chest, please don't hesitate to contact me at aliandeenterprise@gmail.com, I'd love to hear from you. Also, if you'd like to keep up with the Still Here movement please check out my website **Ali Ande Enterprise** at www.aliandeenterprise.com to find out about upcoming events, speaking engagements, book tours, merchandise, and much more.

Here's to life throwing us lemons and us sitting back and using those lemons to make lemonade! I love you all and wish nothing but the best for you on your continued journey.


Love,

Alishia *"Ali Ande"* Anderson

# About the Author

# Atishia Anderson

Has always looked at life with a glass half-full perspective. But, when she lost her first-born son (DJ) it rocked her to her core. Through her journey of love, loss, and triumph she has grown spiritually, rediscovered her purpose, and has become a better wife, [rainbow] mother, and mentor to other mothers and baby loss families who have been dealt the same tragic plight of loss.

It is Alishia's mission through this book (Still Here and other future endeavors) to touch 1,000,000 baby loss families around the globe by creating a community and safe space for honest transparent dialogue surrounding the taboo topic of pregnancy/baby loss (i.e. miscarriage, stillbirth, neonatal death, SIDS, or infant loss) while offering faith, dealing hope, and projecting light into the dark cervices of loss.

Alishia is a stillbirth survivor, the loving wife of Derrek Anderson, the angel mommy to Derrek Jerrell Anderson Jr., and the rainbow mama to Grayson Derrek Anderson. Alishia is a lover and believer of Christ and a self-proclaimed optimist. She is a Michigander now residing in Carson, California and a proud graduate and alumna of both Florida Agricultural & Mechanical University (FAMU) in Tallahassee, FL (receiving a B.S in Industrial Engineering) and Kennesaw State University in Kennesaw, GA (receiving a B.A in Apparel Textile Technology).

Made in the USA
Middletown, DE
01 September 2021